I0154077

MILITARY
SEXploitation

A Lost SOULdier—
One of Many

ELIZABETH E. STIRLING, ED.M

Mystic Tree Fox Publications

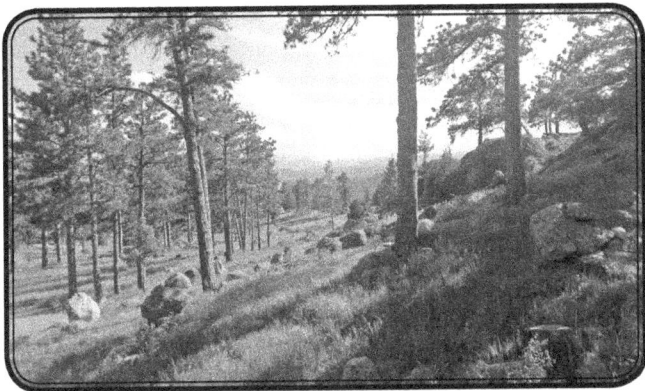

Opening Vista of The Snow and Cloud Covered Rocky Mountains

DISCLAIMER:
This book is based on a true story. The names, dates, and places have been changed to protect the individuals involved in this story. The facts of this story remain the same. Any similarities are strictly a coincidence and are not intended to harm anyone.

PERMISSIONS:
No part of the content of this story is allowed to be copied or used in any way accept with direct express permission of the author of this book.

The Author's Courageous Black Cat Mookie

DEDICATION

This book is dedicated to the courageous men and women in the US Armed Forces who suffer from and struggle with military sexual trauma-related post-traumatic stress disorder. This book is also dedicated to all the soldiers who have gone before and who follow afterward.

TABLE OF CONTENTS

ACKNOWLEDGMENTS

To my wonderful husband, "Charlie," who loves me unconditionally and tirelessly supports me in having the courage to stand in my own truth and to share my story with the world.

For my "dad," who believes in me and never gave up on giving me constant reminders to write my story and share it with the world.

For "Archangel Michael" who enlightened me with the courage to stand in my own truth

For "Archangel Gabriel" who was the guiding light in directing and writing my story

For Archangel Raphael" who guided me in the courage to heal from my trauma

For "Archangel Uriel" who was the overseer of the details in my story

For "Theresa," who encouraged me and never stopped believing in me

For "Wanda," who inspired me to write my story and to move it out of my Soul

For "Ed," who inspired me "to see the light" in my story to help other people

FOREWORD

This book begins with a very personal and highly traumatic experience of a newly enlisted young female US Army soldier. The events, names of the people, soldiers, some of the places, and dates have been changed to protect the privacy of those who were involved in this experience.

This book is based on a true story about what happened to a young woman in the US Army during the Cold War Era in the 1980s. Highlighted in this story are the true events that expose the dark side of US Army culture, sexual exploitation, forced sexual servitude, and rape, to include the use and abuse of alcohol, drugs, and dysfunctional patterns of behavior on the part of some noncommissioned officers (E-5 to E-7) in positions of power over and above the enlisted soldiers in the Ranks of E-1 through E-4. Very explicit, descriptive experiences are emphasized on the part of female soldiers who lived through sexual exploitation, forced sexual servitude, sexual harassment, sexual abuse, intimidation, stalking, and rape while in the US Army. Also included are interviews with key soldiers and the experiences of the victims recorded during a CID investigation that brought some of the perpetrators to justice in the end.

Finally, this story ends with the long term effects that military sexual trauma has had on this young woman's life for many years after leaving the US Army (and continues to have on an ongoing basis), the military sexual trauma/post-traumatic stress disorder related treatment involved, the permanent scars that she has endured, and how she has grown personally from her experience. This information is published to educate men and women about military sexual trauma/post-traumatic stress disorder awareness in the US Army.

The hope is that more soldiers will feel safe enough to come forward and share their experience, offering strength and hope accordingly. The following paragraph includes the definition of military sexual trauma:

"The definition of military sexual trauma is trauma which develops from the unwanted sexual comments, groping of private body parts, forcible rape, forcible sexual intercourse, oral and or anal sex, and any verbal or physical sexual harassment, and coercion or physical threats from one soldier to another regardless of rank."

The experience of this young woman in the US Army follows.

At the age of eighteen, Julia Ferguson presented to the world as a sandy-brown haired, brown-eyed young lady; she was five feet four and weighed 125 lbs., and she very attractive. She resided with her parents in Upstate Pennsylvania after graduating from high school in late June 1982.

Due to the depressed region of Pennsylvania that she lived in, there were no real opportunities for any kind of future in the town that Julia grew up in unless one went straight into a family business or went to college first. Therefore, the only job she could find at that time was at a local drug store as a clerk where she worked from 1 p.m. to 9 p.m. every Tuesday through Saturday. There was no future for her in this line of work since it seemed to be a dead end. Julia wanted to pursue a college education, yet had no family or financial support in which to do so.

Therefore, on December 11, 1982, on a cold, snowy day in Kellersville, Pennsylvania, Julia arrived at the local US Armed Forces recruiting station to discuss opportunities for enlisting in the US Army. Julia was introduced to a US Army Recruiter by the name of Staff Sergeant Greene. He had her sit down and learn about the process of enlisting in the US Army.

The first step was to take the Armed Services Vocational Aptitude Battery. After taking the ASVAB Test, Julia scored high enough to be offered an entry level MOS as a military police officer or subsistence supply specialist. She had the choice of enlisting for two or three years with a mandatory inactive reserve requirement of four years beyond that. Julia chose to pursue an MOS in subsistence supply (76X XRAY) with an agreement to begin a two-year enlistment on active duty in the US Army on February 8, 1983, to end on or about February 6, 1985. Beyond the two-year enlistment of active duty, this contract also included a mandatory post four-year inactive US Army Reserve requirement.

Julia thought that joining the US Army would teach her integrity, discipline, accountability, and responsibility. She was also told by Staff Sergeant Greene that the US Army would pay for her to obtain a college degree as well. It turned out that the MOS (76X XRAY Subsistence Supply Specialist) that she signed up for would only materialize for a part of her permanent-duty assignment in West Germany. The rest of the time Julia was assigned to "detail," which could be anything from shoveling rocks or scrubbing out pot-bellied stoves to sweeping, mopping, waxing, and buffing floors in the company barracks. This experience was horrible!

One is never told about being shoved into a detail crew to be used and ordered to do whatever the higher-ups want that soldier to do. Technically, without being assigned to a duty station where one is able to work in his or her MOS, then a breach of contract is present. Trying to get legal assistance from the JAGG, or Judge Advocate Generals' Office, is almost impossible. Uncle Sam owns you if you agreed to sign up and enlist in any of the US Armed Forces. One is considered to be "government property," if you will.

Therefore, when one signs on that dotted line, this is a legal and binding document. The agreement is stated as such and one has to do what one is ordered to do no matter what.

No rights and no freedom exist for any soldier. One is not able to quit and leave the US Armed Forces without being considered AWOL, or absent without leave, having no granted permission to leave and get out of the service. However, each soldier, regardless of rank is granted up to four weeks of paid leave each year. One must put in a request with the company officer for approval to take leave. Therefore, one has to follow the rules or get kicked out of the US Armed Forces. Ignorance is bliss to the soldiers in the US Military: "Don't talk, don't trust, and don't feel."

As a newly enlisted soldier, one is supposed to be able to trust their superiors and to expect decent and fair treatment. Newly enlisted soldiers, in general, have no idea about the dark side of the US Army. The dark side includes gross exploitation and sexual abuse, rape, stalking, and/or sexual harassment of both men and women that happens in many of the units in the US Army.

CHAPTER I

INDOCTRINATION INTO THE US ARMY

Once enlisted in the US Army in early December 1982, next, Julia was expected to meet with and to be escorted by her recruiter, SSG Greene, to the military entrance processing station in Trexton, Pennsylvania, on February 8, 1983. Instead, on the way out there, SSG Greene drove Julia out into the woods where she could not escape. She noticed that they were in a completely wooded area with no open road in sight!

At that time, he forced her to have sex with him in his car! Julia was very young, very vulnerable, and very naïve to the ways of the world. Julia was told by her recruiter, Staff Sergeant Green, Rank E-6, that her enlistment in the US Army was her only chance to make something out of her life. He took advantage of her as he was in a position of power and used it as a means to enforce control over her as a new recruit. Julia felt violated by him. She felt totally scared and ashamed as he physically attacked her with his hands around her throat, almost ripping off her shirt and telling her to take off her pants or that he would strangle her and leave her for dead in the woods! So, in total shock and shaking, Julia did as he said as she was in fear of her life! Julia was totally powerless with no way out of the situation.

After sexually abusing her and raping her, he treated her like garbage to be thrown out. The "survivor" in Julia kicked into gear as the only way she could deal with the present situation. Julia was told by SSG Greene, "Don't tell anyone, or I will see to it that you pay dearly for it. Hurry up and get yourself to look presentable!"

After they each got out on separate sides of the car to relieve themselves, SSG Greene drove Julia to the MEPS station, which is the acronym for military entrance process-ing station, to go on to Fort David, New Mexico, to basic training with all of the other recruits who were entering into the US Army at the same time.

On the way there, Julia felt scared of the whole ordeal. She said to SSG Green, "I don't want to join the US Army!" At this point he yelled, "Guess what, young lady, you are shit out of luck! You signed on the dotted line, and therefore, YOU WILL GO TO THE MEPS STATION AND ON THROUGH

THIS MILITARY PROCESSING. YOU JOINED THE US ARMY AND UNCLE SAM OWNS YOU! YOU ARE NOW GOVERNMENT PROPERTY! IF YOU BACK OUT NOW, I WILL LEAVE YOU HERE AND YOU WILL HAVE TO CRAWL HOME!"

SSG Greene yelled, "YOU WILL ALSO BE CONSIDERED AWOL FROM THE US ARMY!" Julia cried and said nothing back to him. She was outraged, scared, and she felt absolutely terrified and powerless in this situation. She could not believe that a US Army recruiter would treat her like that. He proceeded to remind her, "Remember, don't say anything to anybody, otherwise I will find you and kill you!"

After that incident, Julia attempted to report this rape to the MEPS Commanding Officer, Major Nelson. He told Julia he did not believe her and said, "You are lying to me, Private Ferguson! You are just trying to get out of being shipped out to basic training! Why would you make up such a lie? You are trying to start trouble and get SSG Greene court-martialed! You keep your mouth shut, Private Ferguson, do you understand me? Otherwise you will no longer exist because I will see to it that you are arrested and charged with making false accusations against a noncommissioned officer!"

Julia said, "Yes sir." She hung her head in shame and cried in the bathroom at the MEPS. Julia could not believe the low-down dirty treatment she had received from the highest commanding officer in charge! Julia felt humiliated, degraded beyond compare, and like she was just another number in a cattle herd, having been prodded, stripped, chewed up, and spit out like meat scraps! She felt isolated, afraid, unloved, unwanted, and alone in this horrible situation!

No one believed her and she felt that she could trust no one! Julia had just had her first lesson in sexual exploitation. The US Army already seemed and felt like some sort of cult where one was being brainwashed slowly but surely into a very screwed up and highly dysfunctional way of life. This was considered appropriate to US Army culture and training, as Julia would soon find out.

Late in the day on February 8, 1983, Julia was "shipped out" from the military entrance processing station in Trexton, Pennsylvania, with a train car of other newly enlisted soldiers, males and females. The MEPS Station was a building that looked like a modern-day high school.

The new recruits arrived at Fort David, New Mexico at approximately 2 a.m. Julia began her basic training at Barret Company 6-3 in Fort David, New Mexico, at 5 a.m. The US Army installation looked like an old prison system. The buildings and barracks were old, dark, foreboding, and depressing.

In charge of the platoon was more than one platoon sergeant. One was Staff Sergeant Collier, Caucasian; rank

E-6. There was also another one by the name of Sergeant Pocatello, Hispanic; rank E-5.

Our first several days included what is termed "in-processing," which involves being schooled in military etiquette, military behavior, command structure, rules of fraternization between the ranks, daily routines, military uniform fittings, assigned field gear and equipment, and getting medical health screenings and shots, etc. The buildings all looked like prisons! What a scary situation this was for Julia and several other recruits! This was the most depressing, God-awful place she had ever been to in her life! Whatever civilian clothing one wore on the day of arrival to basic training was what one was stuck wearing for three days straight, with no showers or change of clean clothes. So, if a new female recruit wore high-heeled shoes and a skirt then she had to march back to the barracks in that same outfit with a large backpack filled with uniforms and boots! This weighed about sixty pounds! Julia was smart enough to have worn a nice sweater and dress pants with a set of matching loafers. Really, one should have worn jeans, a sweatshirt, and sneakers instead! Then one is expected to wear the "BDU," OR basic duty uniform.

One of the first rules enlisted men and women learn is that the rank of E-1 through E-4 are only allowed to fraternize with each other in terms of having friendships and relationships as long as one does not engage with one who is married. This is considered adultery according to the UCMJ or United States Code of Military Justice and is punishable by court-martial. However, no one from the rank of E-1 through E-4 is allowed to fraternize (to have a relationship with) with those soldiers in the ranks of E-5 and above to E-10 or higher. These ranks are known as noncommissioned officers and they are only allowed to fraternize within their own ranks. Then there are the officers who stand at the ranks of O-1 to O-10 or second lieutenant and higher up to a four-star general.

These officers are allowed to fraternize within their own ranks as well. The punishment for fraternization for non-commissioned officers and enlisted men and women with soldiers outside of their ranks is quite severe and punishable by the UCMJ with an Article 15 or court-martial (military trial in court). Newly enlisted recruits were "verbally drilled" with not engaging in fraternization with any higher ranking soldiers outside of their ranks. This seemed like a contradiction in terms, given the dysfunction that took place between soldiers.

During her time in basic training, Julia was assigned to KP or kitchen patrol duty with another female soldier for approximately two weeks. During this time, Julia was approached by another sergeant, E-5, in charge of the mess hall who was African American. He asked her and the other female soldier on separate occasions to sneak out at night by suggesting that they ask to go on "sick-call" (to the base emergency room) and then to meet him at his car outside the dispensary on base.

The other female soldier said, "No, I am not interested in you, and I am not going to risk getting into trouble." Julia said, "No, I am not interested in you, please leave me alone." She was scared and felt trapped! He left each of them alone after that. This was the second time Julia was approached by a noncommissioned officer to meet for inappropriate reasons in basic training.

One female by the name of PVT Vickers, African American, was constantly harassed and stalked by a Drill Sergeant Mason, E-6, also African American in 2nd Platoon. She always said no to him and that she was not interested in him. He verbally wore her down, cornered her at every opportunity, and made her feel powerless! One could see it in her face!

After several threats to her about her life, out of fear for her life she finally succumbed to him and started to meet with him after company time. Drill Sergeant E-6 Mason would pick up PVT Vickers in his car and take her to his apartment so he could have sex with her and take advantage of her. PVT Vickers would openly joke about how he "treated her like a queen" once he had her at his apartment. To Julia, the victimization of PVT Vickers on the part of this drill sergeant E-6 seemed really screwed up, yet she acted as though this was "normal behavior."

She was trying to survive through basic training.

Another factor in this process was the drug dealing that went on in the barracks from the soldiers who were stationed there on permanent party assignment. Two male soldiers were in charge of issuing weapons to all of the female soldiers during field exercises. All soldiers were issued the traditional M-16 rifle. The two male soldiers also sold cocaine and marijuana to the soldiers in basic training as well. At night, between bed checks which took place every 2 hours by one of the drill sergeants, two of the female soldiers in our unit in basic training would roll a couple of joints or marijuana cigarettes and pass them around upstairs in the latrine for anyone interested in getting high. As long as they didn't get caught, there was no problem. Denial ran deep in the ranks of the US Army. Some of the female soldiers would use cocaine to get through the drills in basic training. There were others who were addicted to Sudafed and methamphetamines as well.

In fact, Julia witnessed a lot of the same behavior toward newly recruited females from noncommissioned officers, who are at the rank of E-5 and above. Similar to the unspoken understanding that takes place in a dysfunctional family, they learned not to ask about any of this, not to talk about anything, not to trust anyone, or to show emotions about any of it.

This pattern of behavior turned out to be a common theme throughout the US Army, which went on for several weeks until the recruits all graduated from basic training at Fort David, New Mexico.

After graduation from basic training in Fort David, New Mexico, in early April 1983, Julia was immediately assigned to Fort Lewiston, South Carolina, to attend quartermaster school in order to be trained in her MOS (76X XRAY) as a subsistence supply specialist. The training, which was self-paced up to twelve weeks, took five weeks from April 1 to May 9, 1983.

During this time, Julia was approached by a very tall African American Sergeant First Class Carrington, an E-7, who was in charge of the subsistence supply training class. He asked Julia and three of the other female soldiers to go out with him on separate occasions and spend an evening "playing around with him." To Julia's knowledge, none of the females would go with him and each of them made excuses not to do so, such as having to pull CQ, which is also known as "charge of quarters," or going out to the field on a company field exercise or being assigned to extra duty. Therefore, the E-7 subsistence supply instructor left them alone.

At first, out of her own fear, Julia agreed to meet him, but then she realized a pattern was starting to emerge with NCOs in positions of power trying to initiate sexual acts with enlisted females. When Julia didn't show up that night, the next day after class the E-7 NCO became very angry and then he asked her, "Private Ferguson, why didn't you meet me last night? Were you scared?" Julia said, "Yes, I was scared! You are married, and an E-7 instructor." Julia was scared for several reasons: first, he was the instructor for her class; second, he was married; third, he was African American, whereas Julia was white; and fourth, he was very tall (six feet seven) and menacing! He also left her alone after that.

Two weeks after this incident, Julia completed her training at Fort Lewiston, South Carolina, and then graduated with flying colors! Julia was the last soldier in her training class to be assigned to 39th Armored Division USAREUR in West Germany to begin June 10, 1983. Everyone else received orders to be stationed stateside. Julia requested and was granted three weeks of leave to go home to Kellersville, Pennsylvania, to pack her belongings and prepare for her new permanent duty station in the 39th Armored Division in West Germany.

Julia felt scared, yet excited to go over to West Germany because she had never been to many other states or to any foreign countries. Julia was sad about going overseas. She told her mother she didn't want to go to West Germany because it was so far away from home. Her mom just hugged her and said, "Oh, Julia, you are going to love West Germany, as it is so beautiful over there! Don't be scared; it is going to work out just fine!"

Chapter II

WELCOME TO PERMANENT DUTY USAREUR

On June 6, 1983, Julia arrived at Fitzgerald Air Base, West Germany, on a military flight. The transitional assignment station is where she was held with a group of in-processing soldiers for approximately three days. The flight from JFK Airport in New York City took a total of twelve hours through six time zones. Jetlag had some of the soldiers feeling sick to their stomachs! It took a month for them to get over that. The female soldiers were in one barracks and the male soldiers were in another barracks. The first night they all spent in Fitzgerald in those barracks, they woke up to the smell of really bad coffee! The soldiers all took turns pulling "fire-guard" every four hours. This meant that one of hem stood guard on the floor of the barracks that they were assigned to in rotating shifts. At the end of those initial three days, Julia then was "shipped out" from Fitzgerald Air Base with a group of US Army soldiers to 39th Armored Division at Ehrlich Barracks in Metzger, West Germany, where she was held at another transitional barracks for one more day at the 39th Armored Division Headquarters awaiting assignment to her permanent-duty station.

On June 10, Julia received her assignment to her permanent-duty station at the headquarters for the TISA, or troop issue subsistence activity warehouse, in Scheinert, West Germany, which consisted of a detachment of three US Army soldiers from Metzger. Julia couldn't have been more blessed with the location of her assigned duty station in Scheinert, West Germany! What a beautiful place! The German culture was rich with history and cobblestone lined streets, whitewashed cottages, old buildings from World War I and II, and a large farmers market in the town square, along with the many shops and festivals that took place as well! What a warm and welcoming culture this town appeared to have!

At the headquarters barracks in Scheinert, Julia had one roommate named Noreen, who was African American. She was very haughty and acted as though she was above everyone else. Julia did not like her due to her negative attitude, and Noreen, in turn, did not like Julia either, because she did not want any white roommates and she also wanted to have their room to herself. However, Julia really liked the barracks room because it was in an old pre-World War I building. In this room, the ceilings were very high and the room itself was massive, with tall, deep windows, three beds, three dressers, and three wall lockers. Since there were only two soldiers in the room they each had plenty of privacy. Julia and Noreen also had a hotplate to cook meals on and a mini refrigerator to keep drinks and cold cuts in as well. At one point, Julia even bought a very expensive stereo system and speakers from the post-exchange so she and Noreen could enjoy that.

The next order of business for anyone stationed in West Germany was to attend a four-week local German cultural orientation before beginning work at one's permanent-duty station. This course included learning basic German language and the local currency, which was the German or Deutsch Mark, along with subsequent denominations of currency as well so as to be able to get around town on a bus, train, or taxi. They had to learn the cultural norms and values and proper communication and etiquette while ordering off the menu at local restaurants and in town. The soldiers also had to learn the boundaries at the East-West German border known as "Check Point Kilo," which divided East and West Germany at that time. The soldiers stopped via bus in a town just outside of that known as "Halte" which meant "Stop."

The locals were very unfriendly and did not like Americans. One could see all of the beautiful homes that were directly on the other side of the border wall. It seemed sad that the East German people were not allowed into West Germany due to Communist rule of the Eastern Bloc countries.

"Check Point Kilo," or the East-West German border itself, was quite scary! The large dividing wall in the City of Zurn, Germany, encompassed armed West and East German guards, a live-wired electric fence, and a dog run with highly trained German shepherds! The City of Zurn was the point of entry into East Germany and the other Eastern European countries. The "Eastern Bloc" countries, which included East Germany, Poland, Czechoslovakia, Lithuania, Yugoslavia, Serbia, Slovenia, Bulgaria, Albania, Romania, and Russia, were all under Communist rule until 1989. The only way that one could enter one of these countries was to get an official pass from one's base commander in order to visit, shop, etc.

After the mastery of these cultural norms, the soldiers actually got to visit an iconic German castle known as Lichtenstein Castle. This course, known as "Head Start," was a mini vacation for anyone just arriving into West Germany as a soldier. Once completed, Julia and the other newly assigned soldiers to US Army installations, or "Kascerns," were then able to go to their assigned duty stations to begin work.

In order to do her job as a subsistence supply special-ist, Julia was assigned to the troop issue subsistence activ-ity warehouse about three miles outside of Scheinert, West Germany, as her daily work station. The troop issue subsis-tence activity warehouse was one of six installations that cold and dry food supplies were moved into and out of lo-gistically to support area US Army installations, such as unit mess halls (US Army cafeterias), noncommissioned officers' clubs, and officers' clubs. Julia was given a bicycle by the first sergeant at the HHQ Building to ride to work and back each day.

The scenery in Scheinert, West Germany, and the sur-rounding towns was breathtaking and beautiful! The moun-tainous terrain was lush and green with trees and chalet-type homes with sheep farms and small towns.

Julia (Private Ferguson) was to report to a Sergeant Benson, Rank E-5, who, was age 32 and African American, was to be her immediate boss. His boss was a Sergeant Callahan, Rank E-6, age 34 and Caucasian, who was in charge of running the TISA warehouse to include operation-al oversight of both the cold store and dry store areas of the warehouse. Some of the German farmers worked in and ran the warehouse operation itself. The German farmers also did not bathe or take showers on a regular basis! They had some serious hygiene issues! Their excuse had to do with paying too much for the water they had to use!

Sergeant Callahan gave Julia a choice of either working in the office or in the warehouse itself. Julia wanted to work in the warehouse because she liked doing the physical work, so she was chosen to work in the cold storage with some of the other German farmers who ran that part of the operation. Julia liked the physical exercise.

A German man by the name of Herman Wetzel was the boss of that department. He reminded Julia of a big "Papa Bear" and he was very strict about getting to work on time each day. Julia could not seem to get to work on time as she was expected to ride a bicycle for three kilometers round-trip each day. Julia was then assigned to the dry store area of the warehouse because it was much more flexible with arrival times. "The typical workday in Germany was 7 a.m. to 4 p.m. Monday to Friday except weekends and German holidays.

During this assignment, Julia worked in her MOS for six months at the troop issue subsistence activity warehouse in Scheinert, West Germany. Later on, in December, Julia was ordered by the company Commanding Officer to pack up her belongings and report back to the main headquarters, which was Charlie Company 4th Supply & Transport in Metzger, West Germany. Julia found herself in far too much trouble while stationed in Scheinert. The story behind that follows in the next chapter.

Chapter III

DYSFUNCTIONAL US ARMY CULTURE

When Julia met with Sergeant Benson and Sergeant Callahan, they said they didn't want any women working with them because it meant trouble. At this outstation, there was no US Military oversight from any superiors, who happened to be stationed an hour away in Metzger, West Germany. Since they had no choice, they agreed to give Julia a chance to work with them. Sergeant Callahan asked Julia, "Young lady, I want to see that military file of yours." Not knowing any better to ask why, Julia handed it to him.

While reviewing the file, Julia noticed that Sergeant Callahan viewed and removed the section on sexual harassment from the file. This section was in Julia's and other soldier's military files so any reports of such misconduct could be reported to the company commander. Also, both Sergeant Benson and Sergeant Callahan harassed Julia sexually and made inappropriate comments about her body, which made her feel degraded and ashamed due to the fact that they were in positions of authority. They also made inappropriate sexual comments and remarks about another female soldier to her face, PFC Vickie Faulkner, who worked at an area mess hall at 69th Armored Division in Scheinert. Faulkner worked as a cook in the mess hall. She occasionally ordered and picked up supplies for the mess hall at the troop issue subsistence activity warehouse. PFC Faulkner and Julia occasionally got together to have a few beers in the area, to go to German pubs, and to go out shopping in town on the weekends. She was the only real friend that Julia had at that time. They did have lots of fun together socially when they first got to know each other.

Sergeant Benson was a die-hard athlete who spent most of his time off at the area gym or having affairs with other women. He took Julia out several times and then forced her to have sex with him in his car after getting her drunk on alcohol. He said, "Julia, you had better not tell anyone or I will slap the shit out of you!" Julia found out later on that Sergeant Benson had given her a sexually transmitted disease that she had to be treated for with antibiotics. In fact, the doctor at the local dispensary had to give Julia two large penicillin shots, one in each cheek of her buttocks! Julia was so sore that she could barely sit down! Sergeant Benson then blamed her for this and would not speak to her for over three weeks! Later, Julia found out that Sergeant Benson was actually married to a local German woman, which incensed her to no end!

While stationed in Scheinert, on another occasion several weeks later Sergeant Callahan, who was also Julia's boss, took her for a ride in his car to Metzger (approximately one hour away) to the headquarters at 39th Armored Division for company business on two occasions. He drove them out into the woods where Julia was forced to give him oral sex. He told her to do it or he would make her life hell. He also said, "Young lady, I will deny any of this if you report it." At this point Julia felt like a sex slave. Julia loathed being exploited and used like trash! As a young enlisted female soldier, at the age of eighteen years old it seemed like she was being sexually exploited for the purposes of her bosses' pleasures at her own expense. Julia was in fear of her life at this point. Julia even anticipated thoughts of suicide because of this. Then she fell into a state of depression.

Due to a drinking problem that Julia had developed, she kept getting into trouble by passing out in the bar across the street. For at least a month, Julia kept getting carried in at night by fellow soldiers who would cart her back to the HHQ barracks where she was stationed at Kratz Kascern in Scheinert. Julia kept getting ripped off of her money and her jewelry as well, which to her appeared to be a setup for sexual encounters with the male soldiers.

The barracks that Julia was stationed in encompassed several military companies and a coed dorm type setup where both male roommates assigned to one room and female roommates assigned to one room were next to each other. The latrine or women's bathroom on the second floor was also shared as well. There was a men's latrine on the first floor (where Julia was assigned) and on the third floor, but no private women's latrine.

Therefore, there was a serious lack of personal boundaries as the women had to share the women's latrine and the showers with the men on the second floor! The only difference was a sign that would be flipped to read "men in the shower" when men were in there or it would be flipped to read "females in the shower" if any women were in there. When both males and females were in there at times unknowingly, this got all of them in trouble with the floor sergeant (even though these were private shower stalls and none of them could see each other). This was totally inappropriate indeed!

Also, next to Julia's room, a CID military police officer by the name of Sergeant E-5 Perry Del Mario was assigned. He liked Julia a lot but he was a bit too blunt and rude to her, therefore, Julia only saw him as an acquaintance. He became jealous that she would go out anywhere with her friends and gave her a hard time for drinking too much alcohol. Therefore, he made trouble for Julia and threatened her on several occasions with the words, "Private Ferguson, I'll hang your ass out to dry if I see you out with anyone!"

In late July 1983, Julia dated a military police officer who was African American for about six months whose name was PFC Clifton Foley. On October 31, 1983, they were both apprehended by two CID officers while walking back to the base from going out to dinner earlier at a local German restaurant. The CID officers who apprehended them told them to go to the military police station with them or they would be arrested.

There, Julia found out that Clifton was dealing hashish, which is a form of concentrated marijuana, and that he had been under surveillance for several months. One of the CID military police officers, a Sergeant O'Hanlon, questioned Julia repeatedly about her knowledge of PFC Foley's supposed dealing of hashish. Sergeant O'Hanlon said to Julia, "You had better tell me the truth and admit to your partnership with Foley in selling hashish or else you will go to jail for acting as Foley's accomplice and you will be charged with perjury!"

Sergeant O'Hanlon threatened Julia with being an accomplice to Foley's drug dealing and said that she could be arrested and charged with aiding and abetting a drug dealer.

Julia had no idea that Foley was doing that. He didn't smoke hash around her or even offer it to her. PFC Foley was then arrested and sent to the US Army Hospital Psychiatric Ward in Fitzgerald, Germany, for seventy-two-hour suicide monitoring because he threatened to kill himself over this incident.

During that weekend, Julia went to visit him at the psychiatric ward at Fitzgerald Air Base Hospital. Clifton apologized to Julia for his involvement in dealing hashish and then for getting her into trouble as well. Foley promised to never do it again. Julia forgave him for that. He was later released and sent back to his company at the headquarters building in Scheinert.

On December 12, 1983, PFC Foley was shipped back to his parent company at 39th Armored Division Military Police Barracks at Ehrlich Barracks in Metzger, West Germany. In fact, anyone stationed in Scheinert from 39th Armored Division was technically out-stationed from his or her parent company, which was headquartered in Metzger, West Germany.

Julia was released to Sergeant Benton that night and then brought back to the police station the next morning for questioning. Subsequent to that, the CO of the main company, Captain P.J. De Hart, had to come up from Metzger to Scheinert to release Julia from the police station. They had a brief discussion about the events that happened and he assured Julia that she would be sent back to Charlie Company

4th S&T because she could not stay out of trouble. Captain De Hart said, "Ferguson, I don't even know you and this is not a good beginning in which to meet you as a new soldier with the company! Stay out of trouble from now on or you will surely face more severe consequences!"

Sergeant Callahan was called to come back from his vacation in Fiji, which was halfway around the world out in the Pacific and he was totally pissed off because he knew that somehow Julia would end up in trouble. Anyhow, Julia was really scared and she felt sad because she really loved her assignment and Scheinert, West Germany, as well. Julia had to pack up her belongings by December 9, because then she was shipped back to Metzger, West Germany, to the parent company, Charlie Company, 4th Supply & Transport, where she encountered more trouble than she had ever bargained for. Julia truly hated it there!

When Julia was shipped back to the company, she was assigned to Room 213 on the female floor of the company barracks with three other young women, all of whom were black and hated whites. It seemed like they were always playing classic African American music that one could hear blaring throughout the halls of the barracks. The troops played songs by several popular black musician artists to include rhythm and blues, soul, and pop rock of the early to mid 1980's. This was clearly an African American culture, and it was very different from anything that Julia had ever experienced.

In a word, Julia was not welcome and therefore they did whatever they could to get her into trouble. Whenever Julia was getting changed into or out of her clothes, she heard cruel remarks from one of her roommates such as, "Girl, if you're going to be a sister then you had better act like one!" "Cover up that white shit! We don't want to see that!" Julia felt totally self-conscious as she had no privacy at all in that room and no friends or any support. Julia was mortified!

Julia had also overheard some talk of an E-5 Specialist (female) who was rumored to have slept with Captain P.J. De Hart. Julia had asked one of her roommates if that was true. Instead of telling her the truth, the roommate told Captain De Hart that Julia started that rumor, which was not true.

This got Julia into trouble to the degree that she ended up with a summary grade Article 15, which meant that she was on restriction to the barracks for two weeks. She also had to conduct extra duty every night for two weeks as well. Julia was already in major trouble for having been coerced (under duress) into admitting that she smoked hash by CID and then getting subjected to a urinalysis to prove it. The urinalysis came back false.

Therefore, Julia was going to receive an Article 15 for an incident that she had no part in. An Article 15 is a type of military punishment for minor offenses, which includes restriction to the barracks, extra duty for two weeks, loss of one week's pay, and the loss of rank. At that point, Julia had two Article 15's she had to deal with, to include the loss of two ranks from Rank E-3, thus placing her at the bottom of the totem pole at the rank of private E-1 again. Julia had absolutely no chance whatsoever of being promoted at all! Julia was convinced that she was on a major shit list with a lot of people and that life was going to be total hell for her from now on regardless of what she did. Julia's superiors told her not to make waves because they were watching her.

Clifton Foley and Julia kept seeing each other until February 1984, when he'd had "just about had enough of Julia's drinking problem." He then broke up with her while she discovered he was seeing someone else at the club they used to frequent in downtown Metzger, West Germany. So as hurt as Julia was, she had to get over it and accept that she and Foley were history. Julia and Clifton were not right for each other anyways. This was just as well.

CHAPTER IV

———— ⬿⬿⬿ ————

THE SURVIVAL OF SEXUAL EXPLOITATION

On another note, Julia's squad leader, Andrew Piccard, an African American E-5 specialist, was very menacing and treated her like property but defended her against the male soldiers in the platoon. SP5 Piccard began harassing Julia and expecting her to meet with him for his own sexual favors. She had no choice but to conform to what he expected her to do because it was Julia against him and the other male soldiers in the platoon. SP5 Piccard said, "Ferguson, You are really hot! If you want to stay out of trouble and on my good side, then you will do as I say and meet me when and where I tell you to meet me."

There were only two other females assigned to the 3rd platoon. One of them was already enslaved to the platoon sergeant and the other was almost always assigned to field duty. Julia had no choice but to engage in several sexual encounters and meetings with SP5 Piccard as a survival tool so she could be protected from the other male soldiers who constantly sexually harassed her in her platoon. No one would have believed her if she had reported any of this to higher-ups. Julia had no advocate. She was alone in this crowd of people in the US Army. Julia had no real friends and she felt like an outcast. Therefore, Julia was socially isolated; she drank alcohol excessively in order to cope and she kept to herself. Due to Julia's drinking problem, she could not get her rank back no matter how hard she worked! Instead of getting a promotion, Julia would receive four-day weekend passes to have time off for excellent TA-50 Layouts (field gear) and excellent work out in the field, etc.

In fact, during battalion inspections, Julia, her roommates and all of the other females on the female floor would be bypassed by the battalion commander after waiting until well after lunch. The battalion commander found the male soldiers with dirty laundry, uncleaned rooms, and some of them not having taken showers. Some of them also got into trouble for having gotten drunk and having pissed in the radiators upstairs! They had gotten in major trouble for not being squared away. Therefore, it took a long time for their inspections to end. Thus, the battalion commander had no real concerns about the females because he knew that they were always squared away with having their laundry done, having taken showers, having cleaned rooms and having direct knowledge of the chain of command. Julia and her roommates sometimes laughed their asses off about this! Julia was indeed a marked woman.

On March 4, 1984, Staff Sergeant Albert Smith, E-6, age 34, and African American, entered the picture. Smith was a Vietnam veteran, also having served many years as a Green Beret in Special Forces. He noticed Julia as a new female having just been assigned to the company. He introduced himself to her and said he was attracted to her and said, "I just love that ass!" He begged Julia for weeks to get together with him and she kept saying no. He finally threatened that Julia should meet with him and do as he said or else she would suffer the consequences and that he would make her life hell. At that time Julia had such a bad reputation for being a drunk that no one, certainly not the company commander, would even begin to believe her at all if Julia were to report the sexual stalking, harassment, and forcible rape that went on with Smith.

Eventually, Sergeant Daniel Elwood, E-7, age 35 and African American, entered the picture in late April 1984 as a consort with SSG Albert Smith. Both worked together in 2nd Platoon called the Petroleum, Oil, & Lubricant Motor Pool, or "POL" in the motor pool.

SFC Elwood took over for Sergeant Melvin Zachariah, also an E-7, as the acting first Sergeant during summer in

1984. SFC Zachariah had gone TDY, or on temporary duty abroad, for six weeks. SFC Elwood really got into a power play with anyone who was an enlisted soldier that he did not like in Charlie Company, 4th Supply & Transport. He also made all of the soldiers in the company do five-mile physical therapy runs at 5 a.m. most days during the week.

Elwood and Smith were "buddies" and they were always harassing and stalking the few young women who were of the Rank E-4 and below, like Julia, who was only at the rank of Private E-1 and at the bottom of the totem pole.

It seemed like the stage was being set for the wolves to go after the unsuspecting, innocent sheep and to move in for the ultimate slaughter!

There was such fraternization that became rampant throughout the company that it was a known fact that you did what you were told in the way of meetings and sexual favors with these high-ranking men and some women who were at the rank of E-5. Otherwise, you would severely suffer the consequences, which included severe beatings and death threats. This was also a form of sexual slavery, almost like human trafficking really. These young enlisted female soldiers were told by SFC Elwood to go to "his buddy's house" indicating SSG Smith on different nights, and that everything would be OK as long as they did what they were expected to do, or else "life would be nade a living hell." None of the young women had a choice out to do as they were told or suffer the consequences.

These young women, who were involved in this sexually exploitative culture, if you will, were all stuck in this imprisoned way of life with what seemed to be no safe way out of it unless they paid with their lives!

In May 1984, one such incident was horrific and occurred with Julia and another woman named SP4 Leeds, who was SFC Elwood's pick of women at that time. SP4 Leeds was also African American and married to another E-4 Specialist who worked at D Company next door to Charlie Company 4th Supply & Transport. She also worked in the supply room at the company. SP4 Leeds and Julia were told to meet with SFC Elwood and SSG Smith at 1800 hours one Saturday evening outside the company barracks. They were told, "Get in the car or else we will kill you." Scared, Julia and SP4 Leeds did what they said and they all went to a guesthouse in Rheinhart, Germany.

All four of them filed into the restaurant and had dinner at Julia's expense. Afterward, they had two bottles of Hennessey that they took with them upstairs to two separate rooms. Julia went with SSG Smith to one room and Leeds went with SFC Elwood to another room. They each were forced to have sex with Elwood and Smith separately and then they fell asleep. When they awoke Smith instructed Julia to get dressed so they could join Elwood and

Leeds for a "little fun" with them. All of them ended up in this foursome, which Julia did not wish to take part in

She was told to "get into it or face the consequences." Elwood and Smith were playing with Leeds's vagina and making fun of her. Julia and Leeds were forced to have sex with Elwood and Smith, including fellatio, sodomy, and forced anal sex. Elwood and Smith physically hit both Julia and Leeds with open hands across the face. Both of them were in a lot of pain and were crying for them to stop it!

Finally they both stopped hitting Leeds and Julia and then they got dressed. Julia grabbed her purse and ran out the hotel room door, slammed it shut, and ran as fast as she could down to the German Bahnhof, or train station, in Rheinhart, West Germany.

Julia noticed that she had spent all of her money and did not have enough to get back to the barracks. She waited around for a few minutes, trying to figure out what to do next. A German man named Helmut who was most likely in his thirties noticed that Julia was looking around trying to get a ride. He asked her in English, "Do you need a ride somewhere?" She said, "Yes, but I have no money to offer you for the ride." He asked her, "Where are you going?" She said, "I am going back to Metzger, to Heil Barracks." He said, "No problem, come with me and I will take you there free of charge." He obviously saw this as an opportunity since Julia was pretty much wiped out from drinking too much earlier. Like an idiot, Julia took him up on the offer. So he drove Julia about halfway and they ended up at one of his friend's houses. He said, "Wait here and I will be back shortly."

He spent twenty minutes in that house and then he brought one of his friends with him. They both got into the car and he briefly introduced his friend, "Brent," to Julia in German, and then they drove out into a remote wooded area and demanded that Julia give them oral sex or she would be left out there with no way back! Julia had no choice but to comply so she had to give them oral sex! Julia hoped that they did not have any sexually transmitted diseases! This was the price Julia paid for being stupid and getting into a car with a German man she did not know. Julia was lucky that she was not raped, killed, and left out there in the woods!

In fact, shortly thereafter, Julia found out that these two men were new recruits for what was known as The Red Army Faction, which was a local German terrorist group! After that incident, Julia was driven an hour back to the company barracks and dropped off outside on the street. Julia was in a lot of physical and emotional pain! She is truly very lucky that she survived and lived through that experience, which took place in early May 1984.

At that time, as devastating as that was, an even more gruesome and imminent threat was growing by the day in West Germany. On or about 5:30 a.m. Sunday, August 30,

1984, the battalion commander had all of the troops at Hei
Barracks (which included several area army supply companies) dragged out of bed and told to get dressed and meet in
the company auditorium immediately! The battalion commander made the announcement that The Red Army Faction
was alive and well and had just kidnapped and killed a US
Army 69th armored division 4 star-general earlier that week.
The battalion commander warned them not to go off in any
area, to any Eastern Bloc countries, or to go off with any
company of people that any of the troops did not know because the same fate might await any of them. The Red Army
Faction spoke better English than the troops did and looked
just like civilian Americans and Germans.

Several months later, in October 1984, a criminal investigation was initiated into the fraternization between the NCOs
in charge and the enlisted women, which was conducted by
the battalion commander. This included interviews with anyone involved regarding all of the inappropriate fraternization
that was taking place in the company. During the investigation, several of the young soldiers, as females who were victims of this sexual enslavement, were called for an interview
with the battalion commander. Each of them lied about it
to him because they feared going to jail. In January 1985,
the CID, or criminal investigative division, in Rheinhart,
Germany, took over the investigation because another soldier
by the name of Jared Beck filed a complaint with the inspector general's office about the perceived special treatment of

some of the enlisted females E-1 to E-4, and the parading of them by the higher ranking noncommissioned officers involved. Several individuals were called into be questioned by the CID officers in Rheinhart, Germany. SP4 Carol Leeds was among the first individuals to be called in to answer questions about what happened during this incident.

The Coerced Statement of SP4 Carol Leeds with the CID follows:

I, SP4 Carol Leeds, **WANT TO MAKE THE FOLLOWING STATEMENT UNDER OATH:**

Q. SP4 Leeds, are you now willing to truthfully answer all questions posed to you concerning this investigation?

A. Yes.

Q. SP4 Leeds, have you been forced to make this statement by either threats or promises?

A. No.

Q. SP4 Leeds, have you been advised that anything you say will not be used against you in any criminal proceedings and that a grant of immunity will be given to you on 17 Jan 1985?

A. Yes.

Q. SP4 Leeds, have you engaged in sexual intercourse with SFC Elwood?

A. Yes.

Q. In your own words will you relate to me the circumstances surrounding your sexual contact with SFC Elwood?

A. I think it was in April. I was working in the supply room and I was mad that day at my husband because we got into an argument the night before. SFC Elwood came in to get some supplies and then we just started talking. He asked me why I was looking so mad. He was telling me that I don't need a man to keep me mad all the time. We started talking on a regular basis at that time. We became friends and then one day we just went to lunch at a guesthouse. Elwood paid for a room the first time so we could have sex. Then we started kissing and he was helping me take off my clothes. Then we started taking off his. After he took off his clothes I got scared because he had a very large penis. Then he told me I had nothing to be scared about so I slept with him. He started kissing me all over my body and then he put his penis inside of me. We had sex until about 2300 that night. So then we washed up and he took me home. Then every time he came into the supply room he would wink or try to feel me up.

Q. You stated that you had sex until 2300 that night. How many times that day did you engage in sexual intercourse?

A. Twice. The rest of the time we drank beer.

Q. Did SFC Elwood perform oral sex with you?

A. No, he didn't. I did with him because he asked me to do so.

Q. Were you forced to have sex with SFC Elwood that day?

A. No.

Q. Did SFC Elwood coerce or force you to perform oral sex on him?

A. No.

Q. Was this the only time you engaged in sexual intercourse with SFC Elwood?

A. No. The next time was at the same guesthouse. I don't know the name of it. I just know where it is at. It was me, Ferguson, SSG Smith, and Elwood. They came and picked me up at my house and then we went to the guesthouse. We ate lunch and Ferguson bought her own and SSG Smith's food and room. I bought me and SFC Elwood's food and he bought the room. We all ate lunch and went to the separate rooms. Me and SFC Elwood started kissing again and then had sex again and again and again. Then I got bored and so we went down to Ferguson's and SSG Smith's room. When we got into the room SSG Smith took the covers off him and Ferguson and then I started laughing. Then SSG Smith pushed me on their bed and he said, "Let's have some fun." So I took off my bra, I took off my blouse, and SSG Smith started talking about how big my breasts were. So I took off my shorts and panties and SFC Elwood and SSG Smith came over to me on the bed and just started staring at me. SFC Elwood started playing with me. He was putting his finger inside my vagina. Then he put his penis inside me again in front of Ferguson and SSG Smith.

Ferguson went downstairs to get some drinks and then she came back up to the room. SSG Smith was telling Ferguson that she should not drink so much. Then she just drank both of these tall glasses of liquor. Oh yeah, SFC Elwood started playing with me again, started feeling my breasts. Then Ferguson looked at me and SFC Elwood and she said that it looked like fun. She came toward me and I jumped off the bed. Then SFC Elwood was going to get some more beer so Ferguson said that she was going to go get something to drink. When she left, SSG Smith came to me on my side of the bed and started to feel my breasts. Then he stuck his penis inside me, and that only lasted two minutes. He got soft. So I went back up to my own room. I met SFC Elwood on the way up in the hallway so we went back up to the room. Then we had sex again. He said something that made me mad, so I left the room. He caught up with me in the hallway and told me to stay there with him so we went back into the room and went to sleep. I woke up about five o'clock. Then we went back downstairs to get SSG Smith and Ferguson. SSG Smith said that she did not come back so they dropped me back off at my house.

Q. Were you forced in any way to at any time to have sex with SFC Elwood?

A. Oh yeah, he slapped me, and that's why I got mad.

Q. Why did he slap you?

A. He just kept bragging about how good he was in bed and I told him he wasn't that good and he slapped me. Then he started apologizing to me.

Q. Was this the last time you had sex with SFC Elwood?

A. No. I can't remember when. We were in Ferguson's room and we were drinking beer, then SSG Smith told Ferguson to give him some this last time so she started taking off her clothes in front of me and SFC Elwood. I was going to leave and then SFC Elwood pulled me over to the other side of the room. Then he started taking my pants off. Then he took his off and then we had sex on the extra bed in that room. This was in May 1984. The next time I saw him I told him that I didn't want to be bothered with him anymore.

Q. Were you forced in any way to have sex with Elwood on this occasion?

A. I was kind of scared at first to be doing that in front of SSG Smith and Ferguson. Elwood told me I shouldn't be scared so I had sex with him right then and there.

Q. Did SFC Elwood or SSG Smith perform oral sex on you at any time?

A. No, they were just looking at my vagina, up inside of me. I was sitting on the edge of the bed; SFC Elwood stuck his finger up in there and was playing with me. Smith was just looking at me. This took place in the guesthouse.

Q. Did SFC Elwood have sexual intercourse with any other female soldiers in your unit?

A. I haven't seen it. I have heard of it. I had heard that he went to bed with PFC Mackey and SGT Butler and that is all I had heard about that.

Q. Are you married?

A. Yes.

Q. Where did you get married?

A. Fort Lewiston, South Carolina.

Q. When did you get married?

A. June 30, 1982.

Q. What is your husband's name?

A. Benjamin Robert Leeds. He is at D Company, 4th Supply & Transport on Emery Barracks in Metzger, West Germany.

Q. Did SFC Elwood attempt or want to have sex with you, Ferguson, Smith, and himself all at once in the guesthouse?

A. Yes. It was SSG Smith who said, "Let's have some fun!"

Q. What makes you think that SFC Elwood wanted to have a foursome at the guesthouse?

A. It was SSG Smith who told SFC Elwood to get some of Ferguson. Then SFC Elwood said, "Yes, I want some of it."

Q. Do you know anything about a video?

A. I heard Ferguson tell me something about a video. She said that they had a video of us in the guesthouse. Then Elwood said that the video was of Ferguson and Smith at Butler's house.

Q. Has SFC Elwood ever threatened you if you spoke with CID or the 15-6 officer?

A. Yes. We were told we could not speak to each other about it.

Q. Have you been threatened or coerced in any way by anyone not to speak to CID or the 15-6 officer in reference to this investigation?

A. Yes. When the investigation was going on SFC Elwood told me and Ferguson not to say anything. He said, "Don't tell them anything." He told us that if we tell on him that we would get into trouble as well and that he would kill us to include our families.

Q. When you were first interviewed by Special Agent DeFazio and me why were you so frightened?

A. I don't know. I thought I was going to go to jail.

Q. Did Special Agent DeFazio explain to you that you are not going to go to jail?

A. Yes.

Q. Were you in any way forced to make this statement?

A. No.

Q. Why have you decided to make this statement now?

A. I kept getting harassed and I wanted it to stop. I just wanted to get away from all of this. The investigation is hurting so many people and I just wanted it to end and to be over with. My husband and I talked about it and he told me to tell the truth. SFC Elwood just kept promising me so many things so I would go to bed with him.

Q. Do you feel that what SFC Elwood did was wrong?

A. A lot of things he did were wrong. I just wish he never came to our unit.

Q. Why did you willingly take part in the incidents under investigation?

A. Because I was angry with my husband.

Q. Do you have anything to add to this statement?

A. No.

END OF STATEMENT

Sergeant Smith was married to a German woman who was local to the area. Sergeant Elwood was also married to a woman who was an E-7 in another part of 39th Armored Division in West Germany in the US Army. .

At this point Julia had three new roommates. One was white and the other two were black. Her newly charged roommates were all very aware of this process and were afraid to say anything due to the death threats that they received from SFC Elwood and SSG Smith Beginning in midsummer, one of Julia's roommates, who was black, Private First Class Candace Bula, was a good friend to her for a long time. PFC Bula was already engaged to be married to a staff sergeant at another company in Metzger, Germany. Therefore, SSG Smith and SFC Elwood knew her fiancé and left her alone.

Another female soldier who was relatively new to the unit was also sleeping with SSG Smith at his command. This person was SP4 Page, also black. She knew that SSG Smith was married and stalking several of the females, both black and white. SP4 Page was also pregnant and very hypocritical toward Julia. In fact, Julia asked her several times, "Who do you think you are, SP4 Page? You have a lot of nerve judging me! Stop playing the stove calling the kettle black!"

SSG Smith was more discrete with SP4 Page because she lived in an apartment below SGT Salter. Julia had no knowledge of SSG Smith's involvement with SP4 Page until she openly acknowledged that she had been doing so with

him all summer long in 1984. SP4 Page was never impli-
cated or questioned by any of the CID officers either. Julia
was shocked to find out at the end of this CID investigation
just how many women both SSG Smith and SFC Elwood
had prostituted and victimized!

Also on her floor at Charlie Company, 4th Supply &
Transport, Heil Barracks, was a fairly new Sergeant E-5
Glenda Moussette. Sergeant Moussette was also a lesbian
and everyone knew it. She happened to be the new female
floor sergeant, so she was able to call a GI party, which
meant cleaning the barracks at any time during the week or
on weekends. She also used her power to exert control over
the females on the floor. At one point she cornered and told
Julia to meet her in the private one-bedroom suite that she
was stationed in down the hall. Julia did as she said, and
unfortunately was told to give Sergeant Moussette oral sex
in her private room or else face the consequences. Julia felt
violated and ashamed to be victimized once again!

One evening at the NCO club across the base, several
soldiers were drinking, including several sergeant E-5s who
were getting drunk. Sergeant Moussette was getting drunk
and had run out of money, so she decided to go rummag-
ing through the purses of the women recruits who had left
them at the tables and take their money! Julia almost was a
victim of that, except Sergeant Moussette was caught by her
roommate PFC Candace Bula, who confronted her with that!

Candace said, "Hey Ferguson, Sergeant Moussette is about to take your money out of your pocketbook!" Well, Julia confronted her and said, "Sergeant Moussette, get out of my pocketbook! What are you doing?" Sergeant Moussette said to Ferguson, "I thought you just told me I could borrow some money!" Julia said, "I said no such thing to you! You are drunk! Stay out of my pocketbook!"

With that, Julia had the barkeep take her pocketbook and stash it under the bar at the NCO club until they all left for the night. The next day, Sergeant Moussette did not remember this incident because she had gotten too drunk, and she attempted to deny it. Therefore, several other females confronted her with doing that and threatened to turn her in to the company commander if she ever did that again! Sergeant Moussette apologized to everyone and knocked off the power play regarding the sexual demands of Julia and a few other new females, and she lightened up on having the females constantly engaged in the GI parties after that as well.

Due to the fact that Sergeant Moussette was lesbian, she did not wish to attract trouble from anyone. She had already gotten away with forcing some of the females to perform oral sex on her when she had used her rank of E-5 to abuse her power and to promote fear in these women.

In Julia's opinion, Sergeant Moussette should have been brought in for questioning by the CID officers, charged, and held accountable for her part in the sexual enslavement and ongoing abuse of the enlisted females on the female floor in the barracks. She was never held accountable for any of her part in this ugly mess! Sergeant Moussette should have been charged for abuse of power and rank as a sergeant E-5, coercion, sexual abuse, and enslavement, and then dishonorably discharged from the US Army for her reprehensible behavior and abuse of power respectively.

Chapter V

THE VICTIMIZATION OF ENLISTED FEMALE SOLDIERS

Julia's newest roommate, PFC Mackey, was also a part of this sex-slave operation. PFC Mackey was also made to look like a fool in formation while in 2nd Platoon by SFC Elwood because she initially refused to go along with their scheme. After getting threats and being forced to "get in the car" by SFC Elwood and SSG Smith, PFC Mackey did as she was told. Initially, another high-ranking NCO by the name of SSG Linn was stalking PFC Mackey and commanded her to "get into his car" and go with him or else "suffer the consequences." She suffered being sexually enslaved at his hands, along with Elwood's and Smith's.

It turned out that PFC Mackey was also forced to have sex with SSG Smith, unbeknownst to PVT Ferguson. PFC Mackey was horribly sexually exploited, along with PVT Ferguson and SP4 Leeds. In fact, Staff Sergeant Linn, E-6, would call Mackey "My Princess!" He would tell her to get into his car and go for a ride with him or else face the consequence. She hated that and she wanted nothing to do with these perpetrators!

PFC Mackey's Statement with CID follows:

I, PFC Lisa Mackey, **WANT TO MAKE THE FOLLOWING STATEMENT UNDER OATH:**

On Aug, 3, 1984, I arrived at Charlie Company in Metzger, Germany. I was told that my Platoon Sergeant would be SFC Elwood and that he had a bad reputation. I was told this by SP4 Biggs, who departed to the states a long time ago. He stated that Elwood tries to sleep with all the females in the company, and that I should be careful with him. He also told me that if I don't do as they say, they would dog me out and make life hard for me. I was not put to work for about two weeks because of my in-processing.

When I went down to the POL yard the first day, I was cutting grass and things like that. I told SFC Elwood that I was allergic to grass and he told me that he would give me mouth-to-mouth resuscitation if I passed out and then I told him that I would rather die. He asked why I had said that and I told him that I heard some things about him. He insisted that I tell him what I had heard. I told him that I had heard about him wanting to go to bed with all the females assigned to the unit and that if they didn't go to bed with him that he would treat them badly. He then tried to tell me that it was not true and that people said those things about him because they are jealous of him.

Then SGT Butler started inviting me over to her apartment for dinner. When I went to dinner the first time, SSG Smith, SFC Elwood, SSG Linn, and SGT Butler were present. After we ate they had a lot of beer and the music was on and they were watching pornographic videos and it was like a party. They were dancing and doing the POL Yard Dog. Then SGT Butler was sitting on SFC Elwood's lap on the couch and they were kissing. Then it got really late and everyone was really drunk and I said it was time for me to go back to the barracks.

SGT Butler said nobody was going anywhere because everyone had too much to drink and she suggested that I sleep on the couch with SSG Smith. She and SFC Elwood slept in her room. I slept on the couch with SSG Smith but he never tried to make a pass at me. SFC Elwood always said that I was like a sister to him and that if I were nice to his friend (meaning SSG Smith) then everything would be OK. That's just about it. The next morning they took me back to the barracks and SGT Butler invited me over to her house for dinner a couple of more times, but nothing else was said because I told her that I was not interested. One night after I had dinner at SGT Butler's house I asked SSG Smith to give me a ride back to the barracks. This was about 2300. SSG Smith was giving me a ride back to the company. While I was getting into his car, Ferguson was getting out of some other guy's car (SSG Aaron) and started heading for SGT Butler's house.

SSG Smith called out to Ferguson and told her to get her ass into the car. I sat in the back seat, and on the way to the company. SSG Smith and Ferguson argued about some guy that she had kissed and he told her that she should not kiss anyone but him and he was yelling at her and she was crying. She told him that it was just a little kiss and that she did not mean anything by it. The last thing that he told her was that if she needed anything that he was the one she was to come to for it and that she did not need to go to anyone else for anything. He then dropped me off and departed with Ferguson.

I spoke with Ferguson in my room one night in September 1984 and we were talking about different things and she told me that she and SSG Smith, SP4 Leeds, and SFC Elwood were at a hotel room and that they were forced into having a foursome. She told me that SSG Smith "was big" meaning that he had a large penis.

I asked her how she knew that, and she told me that she was forced to give SSG Smith "fellatio." That's about all I can remember that we talked about.

Q. While you were at SGT Butler's house and they were showing pornographic videos and kissing, did SFC Elwood or SSG Smith ever remove their clothes?

A. No, all they did was kiss and he would touch her breasts and butt while she was sitting on his lap. Usually when he was touching her breasts he would place his hand under her blouse, but SGT Butler never placed her hands inside SFC Elwood's clothing.

Q. Did SGT Butler ever relate to you that she was having an affair with SFC Elwood?

A. She always told me that he was her baby and referred to him as her sweetheart and it was pretty obvious that they slept together because he would go with her into her bedroom at night and not come out until the next morning.

Q. Did SGT Butler ever ask you to do anything with SFC Elwood?

A. She asked me once to kiss him and I thought it was strange because they were lovers and she kept insisting that I kiss him and I refused.

Q. Did PVT Ferguson ever tell you that she was in a film or video?

A. She never told me that, but I had heard rumors about it. I heard that she made a video, the pornographic type. Some of the guys in the company, I don't remember who, told me that they had seen this video.

Q. Do you know of anyone in the unit receiving special favoritism from SFC Elwood or SSG Smith in return for sexual favors?

A. No, not that I know of.

Q. Were you ever offered special treatment in return for sexual favors to SFC Elwood or SSG Smith?

A. SFC Elwood just said that if I was nice to his friend (SSG Smith) then everything would be OK. I took this to mean that they would make everything easy for me if I went to bed with SSG Smith.

Q. Have you received any sort of sexual harassment from anyone because of your part in the Unit's 15-6 investigation?

A. Not since the investigation was going on.

Q. Is SGT Butler married?

A. She is divorced.

Q. Is SFC Elwood married?

A. Yes, he is, his wife is over here and is an E-7 in another part of 39th Armored Division. I don't know where she is stationed.

Q. Is SSG Smith married?

A. Yes, his wife works at the IG's office of Heil Barracks in Metzger, West Germany.

Q. Do you have anything else to add to this statement?

A. No, I have told you everything I know about.

END OF STATEMENT

SSG Smith threatened Julia not to see any other men and that she was to come to his beck and call any time he wished or else she would face the consequences.

At the beginning of June through August 1984, Julia secretly started dating another staff sergeant, an E-6, Richard Arron, white, who was divorced and stationed in another unit in Scheinert (to try to normalize her life.) SSG Aaron took her out shopping for new clothes at his request just to be nice to her. He introduced Julia to some of his family and friends, and they engaged in outdoor activities such as family picnics, German Folk marches, hiking, and festivals.

At one point, SSG Aaron had gotten into serious trouble and was being investigated for smuggling military firearms out of West Germany. He was told that both Interpol, which are the international police in Europe and CID had summoned him for questioning. He was afraid he might end up in Jail doing time for 10 years over this. Therefore, he offered Julia his personal SUV because he did not know who else to leave it to. Julia suggested his ex-wife "Ellen" who was of German descent, should have this vehicle for their 2 year old son Patrick. Since Julia had no rank, she was not authorized to have a vehicle anyhow.

In August Julia had taken a three-week leave of absence to go home to see her family in Kellersville, Pennsylvania. SSG Aaron took Julia to the airport at Fitzgerald Air Base to catch her flight home. While on leave she had done some soul searching to determine the best course of action upon her return to Metzger, West Germany. It turned out that Julia did want to stay in the US Army and make something out of her life.

When Julia returned to Metzger, West Germany, from her three-week leave of absence, SSG Smith saw Julia with SSG Aaron, whom she had been dating in secret. Upon Julia's return from having gone with SSG Aaron for the weekend to Scheinert, she had just brought her luggage back into the barracks to her room and said goodbye to SSG Aaron. SSG Smith pulled up and stopped the car and said, "Get your ass in this car right now!" SSG Aaron became very angry at that time, drove off in his SUV and left Julia standing there!

After several attempts to phone SSG Aaron at the barracks at his company in the following days, Julia finally was able to reach him. SSG Aaron said to her, "Well, Private Ferguson, you made your choice now didn't you!?" Julia said, "I am really sorry about that and I can explain that incident!" SSG Aaron would not listen to Julia and therefore acted like a hypocrite. Given the fact that he himself was in serious legal trouble, facing possible jail time for an international firearms incident, he refused to show Julia any compassion at all. He would not give her a chance to redeem herself! Julia felt very ashamed and never saw or heard from SSG Aaron again after that.

PFC Mackey was in the car with SSG Smith. He proceeded to yell at Julia and threaten her with, "Ferguson, I told you not to see anyone else but me and how could you be kissing another man in public when you belong to me!" Julia was crying and said, "It was only a kiss, so what!" Smith then slapped her in the face and said, "You come to me for all your needs, do you hear me! Do you understand? I had better not catch you with any other man ever again or I will kill you!" The whole time Mackey witnessed this argument between Julia and Smith. She looked horrified and said nothing. They were then dropped off at the barracks and told to forget that this incident ever happened. Julia truly felt powerless!

The next individual who became involved in this scenario was a Sergeant Butler E-5, who became SFC Elwood's "girlfriend" and playmate late in the summer 1984. SGT Butler was not married. She had her own apartment off-post. PFC Mackey and Julia were told to "get in the car" to go over to SGT Butler's apartment. There, they got drunk and had sex, oral sex, and forced anal sex. On two occasions Butler used her rank of sergeant E-5 and forced Julia to have oral sex against her will with her while they were alone at her apartment. Butler was also bisexual.

In the apartment below her lived a black woman by the name of SP4 Page, who was involved in having sex with SSG Smith also at his command. Julia was also told to meet with SSG Smith at his command whenever he wanted. He would pick her up outside Heil Barracks in the evening and then take her either into the woods or to Butler's apartment. He would command her to have sex, oral sex, and anal sex against her will up until early January 1985. However, Julia was not discharged from the US Army due to her ETS (End of Time in Service) until February 6, 1985.

At the end of the fall 1984, PFC Mackey was also involved with a sergeant E-5 Timmons, who was married, and with whom she chose to have a sexual relationship. She ended up getting pregnant by him and was later charged with adultery.

SGT Timmons was in the process of clearing out for his End of Time in Service. Therefore, he was getting out of the US Army. PFC Mackey was granted immunity for her testimony regarding the entirety of this case and then was granted a general discharge for medical reasons from the US Army in March of 1985.

CHAPTER VI

THE RACIAL DIVIDE

Due to widespread company fraternization on the part of high-ranking black NCOs with mostly white female soldiers at the rank of E-4 and below, the CO instituted a company-wide investigation with the battalion commander, which took place in late October 1984 to determine who was involved in this scandal. Racial tensions were high and a lot of civil unrest existed between white enlisted male soldiers and black NCOs, who, happened to be married and appeared to be going out with or prostituting several enlisted black and white female soldiers E-4 and below.

In late October 1984, Julia was sent to participate in a three-week field exercise called "Re-Forger" in Grinnell, West Germany, with her squad. During this field exercise in Grinnell, West Germany, Julia was raped by an African American noncommissioned officer, Staff Sergeant Gilpin, Rank E-6, who was also married. With his knife to her throat, and having pulled her hair back, Julia was forced to give him fellatio on command and she was told to bend over and take her pants down or she would have to suffer the consequences. He forced himself on her at that point. Staff Sergeant Gilpin said, "Ferguson, I have heard about how available you are! Do as I say or I will kill you!" Again, the survivor in Julia kicked into high gear, so she complied with SSG Gilpin, knowing that if she resisted him, he would kill her and leave her dead out in the field!

When Julia returned, she was told by a 1st Sergeant, SFC Melvin Zachariah, E-7, "Ferguson, if I were you I wouldn't say a damned thing until you get yourself a lawyer through the JAGG Office." SFC Zachariah was the one NCO who liked Julia as a soldier and admired her for her strength. At that point, in late October 1984, Julia was summoned to be interviewed with the battalion commander regarding her knowledge of any of the fraternization that had taken place in the company between soldiers.

Captain P.J. De Hart, the CO at Charlie Company, threatened Julia. He yelled, "Ferguson, I am going to get a warrant to search your room and wall locker if you do not comply with my orders to do so! Don't even try to lie to me Ferguson!" Captain De Hart was hoping to retrieve pictures of Julia, Smith, Elwood, and, Leeds having group sex. As he tore through Julia's personal belongings and clothes, Captain De Hart found nothing but pictures of them at company functions hugging each other. He took those pictures from Julia and then threatened her with the fact that she was about to get "busted for having group sex with these NCOs" and then stormed out of the room! Julia was left with her side of the room in shambles and all of her clothing ripped out of her wall locker. She was devastated and in tears! Her squad leader, Specialist Andrew Piccard, arrived moments later and asked Julia, "Ferguson, What the hell happened in here?" Julia then said, "Captain De Hart started banging in the door and demanding to search my part of the room!" "Piccard then asked, "What the hell was he looking for?" Julia then said, "He was hoping to find pictures of me having group sex with Smith, Elwood, and Leeds! There were only pictures of all of us hugging at company functions!" Specialist Piccard said, "I will have a discussion to find out what this is all about with the CO. Ferguson, you clean up, calm down, and stay up here in this room till I come back this afternoon after formation. Don't let anyone else in this room who does not live here, understand?" Nothing ever became of that incident because there were no such pictures of that.

When any of the soldiers involved was interviewed, they all lied to the battalion commander accordingly because no one wanted to go to jail over this ugly secret of sexual slavery that was taking place in the unit.

The battalion commander and his officers had little choice but to drop the investigation because they were getting nowhere with it. Therefore, they passed off the investigation to the criminal investigative division in Rheinhart, West Germany. They quietly interviewed anyone else who came forward with any information on this case.

The CID, or criminal investigation division, then became involved. The CID special agents, who interviewed all of us said that they had "conducted surveillance" of said activity between all of those individuals who were involved in this company fraternization.

The first two people who reported what they thought went on were born-again Christians who thought that they were above reproach. They only reported the interactions and the favoritism that had gone on from SFC Elwood and SSG Smith toward the females who were E-4 and below.

According to these individuals who reported what they saw and thought to be "unclean and evil relationships," company morale had been compromised. SP4 Jared Beck and SP4 Regina Christo said, "This evil has to stop and those who are responsible will be punished by God for their sins accordingly." Julia thought, "Who do these people think they are? This really is none of their business!"

The Statement of Jared Beck (one of the individuals named) with the CID follows:

I, SP4 Jared Beck, **WANT TO MAKE THE FOLLOWING STATEMENT UNDER OATH:**

About five or six months ago, several females were assigned to our unit. Prior to that there was only one female assigned to our platoon and she was an E-5. About two weeks after the six or seven females were assigned to our unit in Charlie Company, 4th Support Battalion APO NY 09036. Private First Class Mackey had acquired a nice comfortable job in the motor pool as the key custodian. At that time NCOs and promotable SP4s were being sent out to the motor pool to "Hump Hoses." This means that they were carrying four-foot hoses across the motor pool and pumping fuel. PFC Mackey was left inside the office doing nothing. At about that time the morale of the soldiers in the unit was going downhill because females were being treated differently. About two weeks after I had seen this happening, PFC Mackey came in bragging about being called "pretty private." She implied that the NCOs called her that. I mean that she said, "They call me that," and, when I asked who they were, she just said "they."

About a week after that, I arrived in the company parking lot, approximately two thousand yards, and saw SSG Smith picking up PVT Julia Ferguson.

I had noticed that all of this was happening and SP4 Page had come back from her leave in the states and asked if she could stay at my house while she cleared the company because she was being chaptered out for pregnancy. About four days after she had been staying with us she was laughing and joking about some pictures. I asked if I could see them and she showed them to me. The pictures were of SSG Smith and Julia Ferguson having sexual intercourse in the missionary position. Their faces were quite clear in the pictures. Also there were pictures of SFC Elwood and SP4 Leeds having sexual intercourse in the missionary position.

That night my wife and I were going to a Bible Study Group at our church located at Heil Barracks, in Metzger, West Germany. Again, I witnessed SSG Smith pick up Private Julia Ferguson right outside our company. He picked her up in civilian clothes and they drove off in his car together. A couple of weeks later my filed complaint was picked for an inspector general review. I went in and complained about what was happening in the unit. They filed my complaint and three days later I was sent to the field. Julia Ferguson was out in the field and I thought it was only fair to warn her of what I had done so she could turn herself and the others in. She just laughed about it and I did not see her for the rest of the field exercise. When I came back from the field I was told that day to get my stuff and that I was being transferred to D Company because I had earlier requested a transfer due to my job specialty. About a month later, in November 1984, I was interviewed by the battalion commander, who conducted an investigation regarding my complaint about company fraternization between enlisted females and married NCO's.

After the interview, I went about work and I was told that the case had been closed, after which, around Dec 20, 1984, Julia Ferguson stopped me and told me that she was getting off "scot-free" because she was short with not much time left in the US Army. At that time I reminded her that the military can recall you for up to two years to face court. She just laughed. When I spoke to the commander of D Company about the investigation, he stated that he had a bunch of pictures of SFC Elwood, SSG Smith, PVT Ferguson, and SP4 Leeds, kissing and hugging at unit functions. But that was the last I had heard of the investigation until this morning when you called me in.

Q: The pictures you mentioned where SFC Elwood, SP4 Leeds, SSG Smith, and PVT Ferguson were engaging in sexual intercourse, do you know who took those pictures?

A: Mrs. Elwood stated that her husband took them.

Q: Do you know anything about a video or film that was supposed to have been made by SGT Butler and SFC Elwood?

A: I think that is the video that SGT Homer had asked me about. He told me that I had missed a really good flick. We were on Charge of Quarters duty and he told me that it was made of people in the company and that it was really good. I told him that I did not want to hear about it. I said this because I assumed he was talking about the people in our company having sex on film.

Q: Have you witnessed any specific acts of a sexual nature between the personnel you mentioned?

A: No. I have seen Smith picking up PVT Julia Ferguson, but other than the pictures, no.

Q: Do you know where these pictures are now?

A: I sure don't. Mrs. Elwood said that she was going to mail them to the CO.

Q: Do you know where Mrs. Elwood is located at this time?

A: I don't know. My wife had the address but we lost it.

Q: Did Ferguson ever tell you how she acquired the job of key custodian in the motor pool?

A: You mean Mackey? No, just that she had friends.

Q: Who is responsible for assigning jobs in the motor pool?

A: SFC Elwood for our platoon because that was a platoon job.

Q: Is SSG Smith married?

A: Yes he is. His wife used to work at the IG's office.

Q: Is SFC Elwood married?

A: Yes, she called the CO about SP4 Leeds living with her husband and she wanted Leeds out.

Q: Is PVT Ferguson married?

A: No, she isn't.

Q: Is SP4 Leeds married?

A: Yes, she is. Her husband is in my platoon but I don't think he knew what was going on.

Q: Do you have anything to add to this statement?

A: No, I think that it covers it all. If I remember anything I'll let you know.

END OF STATEMENT

On January 1, 1985 Julia was called on to attend a party in Rheinhart, Germany by two black male soldiers. Julia used to party with them along with two other female soldiers at Howard Barracks at D Company in Rheinhart, Germany. When they arrived, there were no other females present in their room. To Julia's surprise, both of them grabbed her, stripped her, held her down, repeatedly raped her and held her against her will. They held her "hostage" for three days in their room at D Company at Broward Barracks in Rheinhart. Julia discovered later that she had been drugged and raped by several soldiers who had inserted a walking stick into her vagina while in that same room. They had pillowcases with holes in them carved out for their eyes, which they wore over their heads while they raped her with this walking stick. They claimed Julia was vomiting outside the window at the same time that they were doing this to her! Julia was horrified to learn this about herself!

Then on Monday, January 3, Julia was taken back to her company and dumped off outside of Heil Barracks in Metzger, West Germany. Julia felt like shit! This was a very low point in her life. Julia had no self-esteem and little self-worth. Julia thought that this was supposed to be her lot in life here in the US Army. Julia felt powerless and helpless over her life and she often entertained thoughts about suicide. Julia was very depressed and felt a great deal of shame about what she had been through in the US Army and how she had been treated by these horrible people! She tried to make sense of it but had no one on her side at all. Most of these soldiers were black, as to where Julia was white. The higher-ranking NCOs were black as well.

Captain De Hart, the company commander, was white, and had already blacklisted Julia as a troublemaker who was in a world of deep shit and would soon get what she deserved at the end of this ongoing investigation with the CID in Rheinhart, West Germany.

The following statements are from the male soldiers who were in the room that weekend:

The Statement of SP4 Steven Searles Follows:

I, SP4 Steven Searles, **WANT TO MAKE THE FOLLOWING STATEMENT UNDER OATH:**

Q. SP4 Searles, do you have any information pertaining to a video that SP4 Biggs had in his possession, depicting sexual acts with members of your unit?

A. Yes, I saw the video, and PVT Ferguson was in it, and she was intoxicated. She looked that way on the film and there was a stick that someone had a hold of going in and out between her legs with it. She was wearing civilian clothes, a skirt, at this time. What happened was that I went into Biggs's room while they were watching the video and I saw the film. I asked what was going on and he stated, "This is the movie we took the other night!" I decided at that time to leave and then Biggs said, "It gets better so you should stay around." The next morning, SP4 Biggs, who had been discharged from the US Army, came to me and said that now they have SSG Smith, meaning that SSG Smith was in the film.

Q. After viewing the film, do you have any idea where this incident took place?

A. In the barracks, in someone's room.

Q. Is there anything else that you could add to this investigation?

A. It's believed that SFC Elwood and SSG Smith are in that film having sex with Ferguson.

Q. Do you wish to add anything else?

A. No.

END OF STATEMENT

The Statement of SGT Michael Stoltzfuss Follows:

I, Michael Stoltzfuss, **WANT TO MAKE THE FOLLOWING STATEMENT UNDER OATH:**

Q. SGT Stoltzfuss, I have identified myself to you as Special Agent De Fazio of the US Army Criminal Investigation Command and have briefed you on the nature of the offenses currently under investigation. With this in mind are you willing to render a truthful statement concerning your knowledge of the sexual activities between NCOs and enlisted females of your unit?

A. Yes.

Q. Do you know anything about the rumored sexual contact between SFC Elwood and enlisted females in your unit?

A. I had heard the rumors but I have never witnessed any of these. I had heard that SFC Elwood frequently visited the female floor after duty hours, and that he along with SSG Smith did have sexual relations with PVT Ferguson, PFC Mackey, SGT Butler, and possibly others. I also heard that he had tried to make advances to a new female recruit by the name of PVT Kowalski.

Q. Who told you of these relations?

A. The grapevine rumor control.

Q. Did or does SP4 Leeds, PFC Mackey, SGT Butler, or PVT Ferguson work for you?

A. They did not and do not work for me. I am the NBC NCO and PFC Mackey, and SP4 Leeds work in the headquarters section of the unit.

Q. Do you know about or have you seen any photographs portraying SFC Elwood, SSG Smith, SP4 Leeds, PFC Mackey, and PVT Ferguson and/or SGT Butler engaging in any sexual acts?

A. Like I stated earlier, the photographs I have never seen, but again through the grapevine, I came to understand that SP4 Biggs of D Company was in possession of these photographs and had them stored in a locker in the Metzger Main Bahnhoff.

Q. Do you know about or have you ever seen a movie or videotape depicting members of your unit engaging in various types of sexual acts?

A. As I said I have heard rumors that there was a videotape. I was invited to see the videotape by SP4 Biggs who transferred to Ft. Sill, Oklahoma, and who had a copy of the video. I want to say that SP4 Jeffrey Pratt of my unit told me this.

Q. Have you been involved in any sexual contact with the females in your unit?

A. No I have not—none whatsoever.

Q. Do you know of anyone who has seen the videotape in question?

A. I know SP4 Biggs told me he made the film and he had told me that CPL Saffron, who is out-processing at this time, was involved in making the film and therefore knows the film exists. Rumor has it that CPL Saffron, SP4 Biggs, and PFC Searles might have all seen the film.

Q. Do you know what is on the film?

A. SP4 Biggs described a bit of it to me. He stated that all the male personnel in the film were wearing pillowcases over their heads and that PVT Ferguson had gotten drunk in one of the male's rooms and that all the male persons involved had engaged in sexual intercourse with her. He pointed out that they had even inserted a walking stick into PVT Ferguson's vagina and utilized it as a male penis. He also stated that one of the person's he did not name had sexual intercourse with her as she was vomiting out the window. He did not say that it was anal sex, however, it is possible. That's all he told me. What I have told you I have not witnessed, but rather was relayed to me by SP4 Biggs or heard as rumor.

Q. Do you have anything else to add to this statement?

A. When SP4 Biggs told me about these things, I don't think he would have lied about them, but then again I don't know it as a fact. I cannot think of anything else now but if I do think of anything else I will let you know.

END OF STATEMENT

Sergeant Stoltzfuss, the NBC NCO, had his office Room 211 on the female floor of the Barracks at Charlie Company across from Julia's Room 213. He appeared to be about as straight laced as one can get. He was however, as Gay as a 3 dollar bill! He was such a hypocrite indeed! He also issued all of the NBC gear to include the gas masks that were assigned to all of the troops in the company barracks while on field alert assignments.

A few times when Julia was by herself in her room with the door closed during the day doing cleaning, washing laundry or organizing, she would hear the First Sergeant SFC Zachariah knock on SGT Stoltzfuss' office door and then after being invited into the office, he made the following statement, "Stoltzfuss, this room looks like shit!" "You need to get your ass in gear and get this cleaned up ASAP!" "You are setting a bad example for our troops!" "How the hell do you expect all of us to go out on a field alert assignment when all of this gear is disorganized?" Stoltzfuss would then answer with, "Sergeant Zak, I truly apologize and I will get on this clean-up ASAP!"Julia would then stifle laughing her ass off in her room across from his office. Sometimes, the humor was just too much!

On Saturday, January 8, 1985, Julia was taken with SSG Smith, SGT Butler, and SFC Elwood to Sergeant Butler's apartment where she was told, "Come on, Ferguson, go on and get it on with Smith!" They all had several alcoholic drinks and forced Ferguson to have sex with all of them and then fell asleep. Butler made dinner for all of them and then Smith and Elwood left. At this point in time Julia was always sad and she knew not what day it was. People took advantage of her on a regular basis. It seemed no one was accountable for anything. However, Julia was held accountable for everything. Life was totally unfair. Julia spent the weekend at Butler's apartment, where Butler took gross sexual advantage of her by forcing Julia to give her cunnilingus several times. Then SGT Butler drove them to attend the morning formation at the company on January 10. On or about that time, Julia started to turn her equipment into the TA-50 field gear supply section in order to "clear out" due to her end of time in service.

Even though Julia had thought about staying in the US Army, she knew it was best for her to get out of the US Army. Julia could not wait to leave. She had three weeks of unpaid leave so she was hoping to get out and leave on or about January 17, 1985. Julia had made about 75 percent progress toward clearing out and turning in her field gear and getting ready to get out of the US Army via her ETS or "end of time in service." As for the CID investigation, Julia thought she was free and clear. Julia wanted to forget about all of the horrors that had happened to her and hopefully move on with her life.

SSG Smith had picked her up to go with him, SGT Butler, and SFC Elwood for lunch on Tuesday, January 13, 1985. SSG Smith warned her not to say anything to the CID officers "about their relationship" because it would most likely "cost him his career" since he had almost twenty years of service in the US Army and the same could be said for Elwood also. SFC Elwood said, "I have nineteen years of service in the US Army and I can't afford to lose my retirement or to get kicked out on a dishonorable discharge."

Both Smith and Elwood said, "Keep your mouth shut, Ferguson! If you say anything about this to anyone at CID or otherwise we will have to kill you!" So Julia agreed not to say anything at all because she was afraid for her life. Interestingly enough, three days later on Friday, January 16, 1985, Julia was summoned by CID in Rheinhart, Germany, which was approximately one hour south of Metzger, West Germany. Julia was told to "get her belongings and to get in the truck" by a Sergeant Homer, Rank E-5, who was the platoon sergeant in charge of "Water Point Supply" which comprised 75 percent of their platoon. Only 25 percent of the platoon was comprised of the 4th squad (troop issue subsistence supply), which was separate.

Anyhow, Julia got into the US Army Chevy pickup truck escorted by E-5 Sergeant Homer. Then she went with him to Rheinhart, Germany to be questioned by CID Officers. At the time while on the way to Rheinhart, Sergeant Homer told Julia that she was in "deep shit" with CID and that she should get a lawyer from the JAGG Office or Judge Advocate General's Office before she said anything to the CID.

In fact, after Julia arrived in Rheinhart, she interviewed with CID Special Agent Wazziori which took several hours. She was held at D Company in a room with a strange black woman, a PFC McPherson, Rank E-3. Julia could not understand why she was not allowed to go back to Charlie Company, 4th Supply & Transport in Metzger, to get any of her belongings. Julia was in need of a shower, clean clothes, food, and a serious rest. Julia was shocked, horrified, and very uncomfortable with all of this coercion by CID.

Chapter VII

COERCION AND PERSONAL TRAUMA BY CID

That was the last time Julia saw any of her roommates, or SSG Smith, SFC Elwood, or Sergeant Butler E-5, until the court hearings, which followed several weeks afterward. Julia was not allowed to go back to Charlie Company in Metzger, West Germany, to finish clearing out her US Army TA- 50 field gear, or allowed to finish packing her things up or to say goodbye to her roommates. The CID officers told her that since she had been discovered being questioned by the CID officers by SSG Smith, SFC Elwood, and SGT Butler, her life was in danger at that point and that she was not allowed back at the home company anymore. Ferguson's roommates were ordered to pack up her belongings.

During this time, a very expensive watch that Julia's mother bought for her was stolen in the process.

PVT Julia Ferguson's coerced statement with the CID follows:

I, Julia Katherine Ferguson, **WANT TO MAKE THE FOLLOWING STATEMENT UNDER OATH:**

Q. PVT Ferguson, do you understand the provisions and limitations of the letter of immunity, which you were given by your defense attorney CPT Minotte earlier today?

A. I read it. Yes.

Q. Will you answer all questions posed to you truthfully?

A. Yes.

Q. What is your relationship with SFC Elwood?

A. A good friend of SSG Smith's.

Q. Have you ever witnessed SFC Elwood engage in any sexual activities with female soldiers of your unit?

A. Yes. SSG Smith did not witness that, but we knew that they were in the bedroom at SGT Butler's Apartment.

Q. Have you ever participated in group sex with SFC Elwood?

A. What do you mean? There was a time that the four of us were in a guesthouse in May 1984. I remember that. All four of us were up there in a room. SP4 Leeds and SFC Elwood jumped in bed with me and SSG Smith. I got up and left and went back to the barracks.

Q. Who were you with and what specifically happened in the guesthouse?

A. I was with SP4 Leeds, SSG Smith, and SFC Elwood. Like I said, we were at the guesthouse, and there we ate dinner and drank beer at my expense for both me and SSG Smith. After that we all went upstairs. I paid for SSG Smith and me to get a room. After a while, SP4 Leeds and SFC Elwood came into our room and they took their clothes off and got into bed with us. That's when I got pissed off, got up, got dressed, and went back to the barracks. OK, like I said about the pictures and video stuff. . . I was too drunk to realize any pictures or videos had been taken.

INTERVIEW STOPPED AT 1843 TO ALLOW CPT
MIOTTE TO CONSULT AND CHECK ON HIS CLIENT
INTERVIEW COMMENCED AT 1850 HOURS.

Q. PVT Ferguson, please describe in detail for me what
occurred in that room in the guesthouse.

A. At 1200 noon, I left the barracks and went to SP4
Leeds's house and later on SSG Smith and SFC
Elwood arrived. We were told to get into SSG Smith's
car or that he and SFC Elwood would have to kill us.
Then we left to go to the guesthouse. Once we got
to the guesthouse we started eating and drinking and
that lasted about an hour and a half. Then SSG Smith
and I got a separate room that I paid for me and SSG
Smith, separate from SP4 Leeds and SFC Elwood.
We went upstairs to our separate rooms. SSG Smith
and I had sex for about an hour. We screwed, I gave
him fellatio, and he gave me cunnilingus. About half
an hour later, SP4 Leeds and SFC Elwood knocked
on our door and we let them in. They took off their
clothes and climbed into bed with us. SFC Elwood
spread Leeds's vagina apart and he started finger
fucking her. After that, I got up, got dressed and left
because I was upset. That's what happened that day.

Q. Did you engage in sexual intercourse with Smith in
the guesthouse?

A. Yes. Then we started penetration and that lasted for about twenty minutes. We took a break I'd say for about another twenty minutes and we started making love again. He was on top of me and it was straight sex. Then SP4 Leeds and SFC Elwood knocked on the door and we let them in. They took their clothes off and got into bed with us. SFC Elwood spread SP4 Leeds's vagina lips apart and started finger fucking her. Smith and I laid there and watched. Smith thought it was funny but I thought it was gross. I got up and they were saying come on get back in bed and I said, "You guys are gross!" So then SFC Elwood and SSG Smith started slapping us around! We cried for them to stop it! I got up, got dressed, and left. They did not even know that I left. I went into bathroom and changed. And then I left.

Q. Have you ever participated in group sex with SFC Elwood?

A. No, I have not participated in group sex with SFC Elwood to my knowledge.

Q. Have you ever witnessed SFC Elwood engaging in sexual acts with SGT Butler?

A. You mean like fondling and things like that? Fondling, yes, I saw Elwood grab her breasts. I have never seen them having sex. Lots of times over at

SGT Butler's house she would be sitting on his lap and he was fondling her breasts! I knew that they were in bed together, but I have never actually witnessed them having sex.

Q. How do you know that they were in bed together?

A. I have seen them walk into the bedroom and close the door and stay in there all night. Plenty of times SGT Butler had told me that they were in bed together. She just said that it was good but nothing specifically in detail.

Q. Have you ever participated in the making of a pornographic film?

A. Not to my knowledge, but I was drunk and had heard that I had been videotaped while passed out against my will, but I did not believe it. I had woken up the next day and felt hungover and sore inside my vagina like I had been screwed to death, but I was so drunk I don't remember anything going on the night before.

Q. Have you been told by anyone that the film exists?

A. Yes. Captain P.J. De Hart, C. Company CO, and SP4 Jeffrey Pratt, administration, told me that I was going to be busted. SP4 Jeffrey Pratt said, however, that I could be granted immunity. I did not believe it. That was back in October of 1984.

Q. Has anyone ever told you that they have viewed the video?

A. No, but that they had heard there was a video and that SP4 Biggs had it.

Q. Has SFC Elwood ever approached you to have sex with his friends?

A. Yes, just SSG Smith because that is his best friend. He would say stuff like, "Meet my buddy tonight, so you guys can have fun." He told me that he would get me out of work early and sometimes out of PT [five mile physical therapy run at 5 a.m.]. He used the generalized term, "I'll take care of you if you do me some favors that I need done." These favors were like taking charge of quarters while another soldier went to a basketball game. Elwood made remarks like, "My buddy," meaning Smith, "wants to meet you tonight."

Q. Has SFC Elwood ever solicited you to have sex with anyone other than Smith?

A. No he has not.

Q. When did you first engage in sexual intercourse with Smith?

A. On the night of April 4, 1984 at his government residential quarters.

Q. Did you know that SSG Smith was married?

A. No, I did not know that SSG Smith was married until this investigation was started, and that his wife was out of town that night. We ate steak and drank some gin up until about eleven o'clock that night. Then he asked me if I would make love to him. We did it doggy style on the couch and it lasted about fifteen minutes. After that we watched videos until about 0230 in the morning and then he took me back to the barracks. Prior to having sex on the couch we both took off our clothes and he asked me to give him head, and I did. After that we started screwing.

Q. How often have you engaged in sexual intercourse with SSG Smith?

A. I can't count how many times. On the average we had sex two or three times per week, different places, such as in the car or woods, at Butler's house while she was in the house, with Butler in the bedroom and I and Smith would be in the living room, not engaged in sex all the time. We would sit down and drink alcohol. There were periods of time, like three to six weeks, that we would spend apart due to the fact that

SSG Smith was assigned to the field and then I might be occasionally dating someone else.

Q. Did SFC Elwood ever threaten you in any way during the investigation?

A. Back in Oct '84, SFC Elwood told me not to say anything about him and Sergeant Butler because they would both end up in jail. He threatened me with coming after me and taking my life if I said anything to anyone, including CID! He said that because he is married and his relationship with SGT Butler would be considered adultery.

Q. Did SSG Smith also ask you not to say anything?

A. Yes, for the same reason that SFC Elwood threatened me not to say anything.

Q. Did SFC Elwood, SGT Butler, SP4 Leeds, SSG Smith, or anyone else threaten you with bodily harm if you said anything to the authorities concerning this investigation?

A. Yes, they did threaten me with, "Ferguson, keep your mouth shut or you will be silenced permanently!" They stated that they did not want to go to jail and that I was to keep my mouth shut or they would come after me and kill me. They would be charged with adultery because all of them are married except SGT Butler.

Q. When you were first interviewed by the CID, why were you so frightened?

A. Because I thought I was going to jail if I said anything.

Q. Why did you first lie to Special Agent Wazziori and me about the sexual relations you had with SSG Smith and the entire circumstances about this investigation?

A. Because I was scared and did not really know what to do.

Q. What made you decide to finally tell the truth now?

A. After speaking with both of you and being honest with myself, I felt that it would be better to tell the truth than to lie.

Q. Why did you render a false statement to the 15-6 investigation officer about this incident?

A. Because I was scared that my life would be in jeopardy and/or that I would end up in jail.

Q. Are you now making this statement freely without any threats or promises?

A. Yes.

Q. What is PFC Mackey's involvement in this investigation?

A. She was having a relationship with SGT Timmons, who is now a SP4. However, back in August 1984 he was an E-5 and married.

Q. What do you mean by PFC Mackey having a relationship with SP4 Timmons?

A. What I mean is hearing the sounds of sexual activity late at night in her separate part of our room. Afterward she told me about it and said that it was good. She did not go into lurid details. She just said it was good.

Q. What is PFC Mackey's involvement with SFC Elwood and SSG Smith?

A. One night—and this is the only night that I know of—she and SFC Elwood and I and SSG Smith all went to SGT Butler's apartment. SSG Smith and I cooked dinner and the only thing I saw her do was kissing SFC Elwood on the mouth and that's it. SFC Elwood tried to get her to go to bed with him and she chickened out because SFC Elwood was already with Sergeant Butler; Mackey was scared. He's so big and she is so tiny that it drove her up the wall just for him to give her a hug.

Q. Did you ever tell anyone that you were forced into giving Smith head?

A. PFC Mackey. I told her once that I was forced several times into giving Smith head.

Q. Do you know an individual named SP4 Biggs?

A. Yes, they claim he had a video. He told SSG Linn that he had a video. One night I was in Biggs's room with him and some others drinking beer and watching TV, but nothing that I knew of ever happened. I don't remember having done anything with them. I thought they were my friends. Then I discovered that I had been drugged and I was totally sore between my legs.

Q. Do you know how PFC Mackey became the key custodian at the POL yard?

A. Yes, because SFC Elwood was trying to get her to go to bed with him. He told me so. He said he gave her the job, "Because I want some of that ass!"

Q. Did Elwood ever talk to you about explicit sex?

A. Yes, He would talk about "I want some of that pussy," referring to SP4 Leeds and SGT Butler. He asked me if my sex with Smith was good, that's it.

Q. Did you ever view any pornographic films? If so where and who was present?

A. Over at Butler's house we viewed some pornographic flicks. I was there with SSG Smith, SFC Elwood, and SGT Butler, who, were together watching. Usually after watching the fuck flicks, they, or SFC Elwood and SGT Butler, would go into the other room, into her bedroom, and SSG Smith and I would stay in the living room. SFC Elwood and SGT Butler had sex and we did too.

Q. Were you in any way forced into performing any sexual acts or participation in any acts by anyone?

A. Yes. I had no choice.

Q. Why did you willingly participate in this incident under investigation?

A. Because I was threatened with being killed if I did not do as I was told and I felt powerless.
SSG Smith told me to do as he said or he would kill me and my family.

Q. Do you have anything else to add to this statement?

A. No, I don't.

END OF STATEMENT

Therefore, Julia could not go back to get any of her things from Charlie Company at Heil Barracks, 4th Supply & Transport Battalion in Metzger, West Germany. Julia was truly horrified by what had happened! She was then held at C Company in Rheinhart in a room with another black female, PFC McPherson, Rank E-3, who, was a major troublemaker and who was also in the process of getting charged with crimes against other female soldiers (such as pouring bleach underneath the doorways of their rooms and attempting to set them on fire!) PFC McPherson was involved in a black sports team with several black male soldiers, all of whom played basketball together at the Base Gym in Rheinhart, Germany. Julia believed that the CID officers created this setup so Julia would eventually talk and tell them what they wanted to hear from her involving the CID investigation.

PFC McPherson was kind enough to lend Julia some shampoo and soap since she had none or any of her clothes or any change of uniform either. Julia went out that evening and got drunk with some other soldiers. When she arrived back at the room, she almost slipped on the wet floor, which McPherson had just gotten done mopping up. Julia said, "I can't believe you; I almost fell on this floor!" At this point she had several of her black male friends in the room with her. Julia said, "Hey, I am really sorry!" She said, "You white bitch! We are going to kill you!" They all proceeded to attack and hold Julia down and beat the living shit out of her by punching her and kicking her, breaking her nose in he process and three of her ribs. Julia staggered and got up, heading toward the door, and one of them slammed her face into the edge of it. Her face was a mess and bleeding as a result of that! Then Julia ran down the hall, screaming, to SP4 Collins (he stood about six foot four), the soldier on charge of quarters that evening, who then went after McPherson and had her arrested by the military police for physical assault!

SP4 Collins, the soldier on CQ, strongly suggested that someone take pictures of Julia's face and that she go immediately to the dispensary to have X-rays taken of her ribs, face, and scull. He had his assistant take Julia immediately to the emergency room dispensary. Julia had black eyes to the point of looking like a bandit. She was interviewed at the dispensary by a male nurse who was very angry at her and asked, "Who did this to you, Ferguson! This makes us look real bad!" Even though the medics said no broken bones were discovered through an X-ray, they would not give Julia a full report of what was wrong with her. They did a cover-up.

Julia was then sent back to C Company with orders to rest for three days and to take aspirin or Tylenol as needed. Julia was in immense pain! Due to the black bruising around her eyes and nose, Julia knew her nose had most likely been broken, which would have been more finely detected through an MRI. Julia was assigned to a room with a Sergeant Patrice, who was very religious and protective. The following morning Julia was questioned by the first sergeant,

SFC O'Brien, at C Company, where she was being held. He blamed Julia for this happening, and SFC O'Brien asked her "How do you think that this makes me feel? Ferguson, you are already in enough trouble! How do you think this makes us look? This makes us look real bad! Do you think this is some kind of joke? You stand outside my office at parade rest until further notice do you understand me, Ferguson?" Julia said, "Yes, First Sergeant, I understand." He didn't give a shit about how Julia felt, whether she was in pain or not, or what this whole process had done to her at all. Julia was still at a very low point in her life and she often entertained thoughts of suicide.

While assigned to a room with Sergeant Patrice, Rank E-5, Julia stayed with her for a week for safety reasons. At her request, SGT Patrice wanted Julia to get a nice dress out for church. The dress Julia had was very nice and more than appropriate. SGT Patrice brought Julia to church with her that following weekend. Sergeant Patrice said, "Ferguson, I have seen the light in you and all you have to do is to believe in God and your life will change for the better." Sergeant Patrice was really the only light in Julia's life at that time and she was a good influence on her in terms of helping her to find hope and to have faith in life. After Julia's assignment to Sergeant Patrice, CID released her from questioning. At the end of that week, Sergeant Patrice said, "Since I am no longer your assigned keeper, you are free to go."

At that point, Julia was then assigned to another room with PFC McPherson's best friend, PFC Rivera, whom she had no desire to be around. She thought Julia was messing around with her boyfriend and some other male soldiers. She then threatened to kick Julia's ass if she spoke to them, so Julia stayed away from them. Julia was allowed to go anywhere she wished on post, but not back to Charlie Company, Heil Barracks, 4th Supply & Transport, in Metzger, Germany.

The CID officers whom Julia had interviewed with regarding the CID investigation informed her that her life was in danger due to her testimony against everyone involved in the fraternization with SSG Smith, SFC Elwood, SP4 Leeds, and SGT Butler. After the abuse from the CID officers and the physical assault from McPherson and her friends, and after the verbal abuse by the first sergeant, SFC O'Brien at C Company, Julia met with Command Sergeant Major Car Hart. She was very much taken under his wing while she was still at C Company in Rheinhart, West Germany. He protected her from the verbal abuse and threats of the first sergeant, SFC O'Brien.

CSM Car Hart told Julia that she did not have to participate in any company physical training runs, and that SFC O'Brien was to leave her alone and to stop harassing her by having her "stand at parade rest" outside his office, to stay out of the CID investigation, and that if SFC O'Brien did not like it, he would have to answer to CSM Car Hart. Julia was then called into the first sergeant's office one more time to see SFC O'Brien about her unwillingness to participate in the company run because she did not have any running shoes. Julia told him about the conversation that CSM Car Hart had with her about all of this, and that he was to leave her alone and stop harassing her about the CID Investigation, or anymore company functions such as PT, GI parties, or standing at parade rest outside of his office.

The First Sergeant got very angry and said, "Ferguson, if you are lying to me, I will make sure you go to jail for insubordination!" SFC O'Brien called CSM Car Hart and asked if any of this were true. The CSM reiterated what Julia had conveyed to SFC O'Brien, and then SFC O'Brien became very angry and dismissed Julia from his office. SFC O'Brien said, "Ferguson, you stay out of sight, out of mind! Do you understand me, soldier!" Julia said, "Yes, First Sergeant!" At this time Julia felt like she had a few caring people in the US Army who were on her side for once and that it was not a totally bad experience.

Chapter VIII

---⊗⊗⊗---

THE OUTCOME OF THE CID INVESTIGATION

On or about February 3, 1985, Julia was escorted to court by a CID officer and ordered to testify at the court hearings. After testifying in lurid detail about the sexual incidents in the investigation, at the command of the military court judge, during the court-martial for SSG Albert Smith, E-6, and SFC Daniel Elwood, E-7, Julia was told to pack up her belongings by the JAGG officers. At 2 a.m. on February 4, 1985, Julia was flown out of Fitzgerald Air Base, Germany, and back to the US to the out-processing station at Fort David, New Mexico. On February 6, 1985, Julia was honorably discharged from the US Army.

Julia was told by the JAGG Officers, before she lef
Germany, that she might be called to testify further in these
court hearings in Rheinhart, Germany

Upon her release from the US Army, Julia was left hang-
ing off of an emotional cliff that she would later discover to
be a major skeleton in her closet. This caused her to suffer
from post-traumatic stress disorder and to wreak havoc on
her life for many years afterward and into the present day.
Julia continued to repeat several of the same old patterns of
survival by virtue of attracting very dysfunctional people,
places, predatory bosses, strange jobs, and situations. Julia
could not understand why her life took such a dysfunctional turn until much later, when she was in her forties. That
is when she was compelled to write this book about her
experience.

Chapter IX

———— ∞∞∞ ————

WITNESSES, VICTIMS, AND PERPETRATORS

PERPETRATORS:

1. Smith, Albert (NMN): SSG; 000-00-0000; 4 April 50; Gadsden, AL; M; Black; C Co, 4th Support Battalion, APO NY 09036; Adultery; Indecent Acts with Another; Solicitation to Commit an Offense (Sodomy); Obstruction of Justice; Sodomy.

2. Elwood, Daniel A.: SFC; 000-00-0000; 6 Feb 51; Gary, IN; M; Black; C Co, 4th Support Battalion, APO NY 09036; Adultery; Indecent Acts with Another; Assault; Solicitation to Commit an Offense

(Sodomy); Inappropriate Video Filming of Sexual Acts; Prostitution; Obstruction of Justice.

3. Timmons, Weston: SP4; 000-00-0000; 5 June 1966 Corpus Christie, TX; M; Black; D Co, 4th Support Battalion, APO NY 09036; Adultery.

4. Mackey, Lisa L. PFC; 000-00-0000; 12 March 1968 Stockton, CA: F; Black; C Co, 4th Support Battalion APO NY 09036; Adultery.

VICTIMS:

1. Elwood, Brianna J. SFC; 000-00-0000; 10 October 1950; Gary, IN; F; Black; HHC 3rd ID, APO NY 09036; Adultery

2. Smith, Susan A. Civilian; FRG; F; White (Deutsch Wife of SSG Albert Smith); 000-00-0000; C Co, 4th Support Battalion, APO NY 09036); (NFI); Adultery

3. Leeds, Carol L.; SP4; 000-00-0000; 13 Nov 1960; Smyrna, GA; F; Black; C Co, 4th Support Battalion, APO NY 09036; Assault; Indecent Acts with Another; Solicitation to Commit an Offense (Sodomy/Adultery)

4. US GOVT; Obstruction of Justice.

5. Butler, Charlotte J.; SGT E-5; 000-00-0000; 26 March 1952; Gary, IN; F; Black; C Co, 4th Support Battalion, APO NY 09036; (NFI); Adultery

6. Ferguson, Julia Katherine; PV1; 000-00-0000; 10 Dec 1962; Kellersville, PA; F; White; C Co, 4th Support Battalion, APO NY 09036; Sodomy; Solicitation to Commit an Offense (Sodomy/Adultery)

SYNOPSIS:

Investigation revealed that SSG Smith, a black married man, solicited PVT Ferguson, a white female enlisted soldier, not his wife, to engage in sexual intercourse with him several times.

Between April 1984 and Oct 1984, at various locations within Rheinhart and Metzger, West Germany, SSG Smith solicited PVT Ferguson to participate in the acts of sexual intercourse, fellatio, and cunnilingus with him several times.

Furthermore, on an unknown afternoon and date, in an unknown hotel in Rheinhart, West Germany, SFC Elwood had sexual intercourse with SP4 Leeds, an enlisted black woman, not his wife. Furthermore, SFC Elwood committed an indecent act upon SP4 Leeds by fondling her breasts in the presence of SSG Smith and PVT Ferguson.

Between April 1984 and October 1984, in an unknown hotel in Rheinhart, West Germany, and in Room 213, Building 306, Heil Barracks, Metzger, West Germany, SFC Elwood, a married man, solicited SP4 Leeds, not his wife, to have sexual intercourse and commit fellatio upon him several times. Furthermore, during this time in the unknown hotel, SFC Elwood, after a verbal altercation with SP4 Leeds, slapped Leeds in her face with his open hand several times. SSG Smith also slapped PVT Ferguson on several times as well. Between July 1984 and August 1984, in Room 213,

Building 306, Heil Barracks, Metzger, West Germany, SP4 Timmons, a married man, had sexual intercourse five or six times with PFC Mackey, a female, not his wife.

Further investigation revealed that at an unknown time, date, and location, SSG Smith and SFC Elwood approached PVT Ferguson and SP4 Leeds and attempted to obstruct justice by soliciting them not to testify against them in an upcoming military proceeding or that their lives would be threatened.

BASIS FOR INVESTIGATION:

At 11:10 a.m., December 20, 1984, Lieutenant Colonel Schwartz, battalion commander, 4th Support Battalion, APO NY 09701, contacted Special Agent Wazziori and related that after coordination with Major Klinefeld, 39th Armored Division Special JAGG Agent, APO NY 09031, that the battalion commander wanted to report an incident which was discovered during an AR 15-6 investigation, where NCOs assigned to C Co, 4th Supply, 4th Support Battalion, APO NY 09036, were soliciting female soldiers to participate in sexual acts and that the NCOs involved were married.

The Statement of SP4 Clarence P. Stuart follows:

I, SP4 Clarence P. Stuart, **WANT TO MAKE THE FOLLOWING STATEMENT UNDER OATH:**

Q. SP4 Stuart, are you aware of an on-going investigation concerning sodomy and indecent acts with another involving SFC Elwood and SSG Smith?

A. Yes.

Q. What knowledge do you have concerning this matter?

A. Around April or May 1984 I had seen photographs of SFC Elwood hugging SP4 Leeds and both of them were fully clothed. I also saw a photograph of SSG Smith and PVT Julia Ferguson hugging each other.

Q. Do you recall who showed you the photographs?

A. No, I do know that they are members of the unit.

Q. What were the photographs shown to you?

A. The person(s) who showed me the pictures said that they were going to get back at SFC Elwood for screwing with him. I believe it was because at times SFC Elwood was openly prejudiced.

Q. Could you give any specifics about the people who showed you the photographs?

A. There were two people who showed me the photographs, both Caucasians.

Q. Did you see a videotape concerning SFC Elwood or SSG Smith?

A. No, however, I had been told by an individual named Biggs (who has since been discharged from the Army) that he had made a videotape showing PVT Ferguson doing indecent acts.

Q. Did you ever view this videotape?

A. No, unless it was one that Biggs had told me he had, however, he never related to me any specifics concerning this tape nor had I ever seen the video.

Q. So you are aware of two videotapes, one of which shows Ferguson performing indecent acts with several people while in the barracks, which was made by Biggs. SSG Smith had told you that they had taken off their clothes and put paper bags on their heads and inserted a walking stick into PTV Ferguson's vagina while she had a skirt on, then she vomited outside the window. The other tape prepared by SP4 Biggs would not say what was specifically on the tape.

A. Yes.

Q. Is there anything else you would like to add concerning this matter under investigation?

A. No.

END OF STATEMENT

The statement made at the time by Julia Katherine Ferguson, PVT E-1, was dictated specifically by the CID officers who interviewed her. She had written a five-page statement of her own personal truth and account of what had taken place over the course of her sexual enslavement by Smith and Elwood. The CID officers stated, "We don't want that statement from you. PVT Ferguson, you will answer the following questions in explicit detail and to our specifications or you will be charged with perjury and sentenced to serve federal prison time at Fort Leavenworth, Kansas!"

Therefore, Julia was coerced to answer the questions in her statement above (under duress) exactly as the CID Special Agents instructed her to do or face the consequences. Julia felt powerless and horrified that her truth was not acceptable to the CID officers! She was ashamed to answer the above questions and to make the above statement under oath in such graphic, lurid, and disgusting detail! Julia had to stand in the courtroom and recite these answers specifically to the officers of the court and in front of a lot of people, with the wives of Smith and Elwood watching and listening to the entire testimony in the courtroom!

Julia was so mortified by this and found herself in a severe state of depression subsequent to that. The above statement was not her original statement and she was coerced under duress by the CID officers to say what is documented

In this report. Therefore it is not entirely true and contradicts what really happened to Julia in some of these situations.

In the military, one is not able to say, "No, I don't want to do that." The consequences are severe with respect to saying no to anyone about what you do not wish to partake in.

When Julia said, "No, I don't want to do that," to the higher-ranking noncommissioned officers, she received physical beatings and threats on her life by them. So, Julia had no choice but to follow orders.

Soldiers are no longer seen as people who are treated with respect, but as just a number, with no personal rights; they are treated like property. Therefore, the higher-ranking noncommissioned officers who are rank E-5 and above can force one to do whatever is commanded of him or her. One is not able to just quit the military and leave without being charged with and being AWOL, or absent without leave. There is no way out, nowhere to hide, and no one will listen to that soldier regarding any kind of stalking, rape, sexual assault, physical groping of body parts, name calling, or belittling. One will just be told, "This stuff happens, so get over it!"

The following statement, which was made by Sergeant Butler, was a lie in that she did have an ongoing sexual relationship with Sergeant First Class Elwood. No one actually saw her have sex with him. However, it was obvious that she did on a regular basis. She also forced Julia to perform cunnilingus on her on two separate occasions at her home while she was overly intoxicated. At those times Julia could not say no and she could not escape from Sergeant Butler. However, Sergeant Butler managed to get away with either lying to the CID officers or telling them a half-truth and then they covered it up so as to obtain information from her for her knowledge of the incidents in this investigation. Sergeant Butler was titled as a victim under the investigation. In Julia's personal opinion, Sergeant Butler should have been listed as a perpetrator, charged with adultery and sodomy, and dishonorably discharged from the US Army due to her abuse of power as a sergeant E-5. Therefore, military justice was not served in this part of the case.

The Statement of SGT Charlotte Butler Follows:

I, SGT Charlotte Butler, **WANT TO MAKE THE FOLLOWING STATEMENT UNDER OATH:**

Q. SGT Butler, you have received a letter from Major General Watters basically ordering you to answer all questions pertaining to this investigation of SFC Elwood and SSG Smith truthfully. Do you fully understand the letter that was sent to you and do you have any questions about the content of the letter?

A. Yes, I understand the letter, and I don't have any questions.

Q. SGT Butler do you know SFC Elwood?

A. Yes I do.

Q. SGT Butler, what is your relationship with SFC Elwood?

A. There's no relationship.

Q. SGT Butler, has SFC Elwood ever been to your apartment?

A. Yes, he has.

Q. SGT Butler, please explain in your own words how many times SFC Elwood was at your apartment and what occurred there?

A. SFC Elwood came up to my apartment when I and SSG Smith and SSG Linn were having dinner and that is the only time I could remember him coming up.

Q. SGT Butler, who else was in your apartment at that time, during the dinner?

A. SSG Smith and PFC Mackey.

Q. SGT Butler, did both SSGs sleep over at your apartment at that time?

A. Yes.

Q. SGT Butler, where did Smith sleep?

A. SSG Smith slept on the couch.

Q. Did anyone else sleep over at your apartment at this time?

A. No.

Q. Did you drink any alcohol at dinner?

A. Yes I did.

Q. Do you recall everything that happened at this dinner?

A. Some of it.

Q. Tell me what you recalled?

A. We just ate dinner and talked about the Army and just drank beer.

Q. Did you sit on SFC Elwood's lap at this dinner?

A. I don't recall.

Q. Did SFC Elwood ever fondle your breasts?

A. No.

Q. While at that dinner, were any videos shown?

A. No.

Q. Do you have a video?

A. Yes.

Q. Did you ever play sex films on your video?

A. Yes I have played them on my video.

Q. While you played the sex films, who else viewed them with you?

A. No one.

Q. What were some of the names of the videos?

A. I can't recall.

Q. Where did you get the videos?

A. I rented them outside Howard Barracks.

Q. Did you ever call SFC Elwood "Baby"?

A. I don't recall calling him "Baby."

Q. Did you ever call SFC Elwood "Sweetheart"?

A. I don't recall.

Q. You have answered several questions by stating that you could not recall. Are you telling me that the answers could be yes?

A. And they could be no.

Q. Were you ever in the Hotel Thune?

A. Yes, while I was TDY.

Q. Was SFC Elwood TDY with you at the time?

A. No, he wasn't, but he did come down to check on my troops and the operation, Eurail.

Q. Did SFC Elwood have sex with you in that room in the Hotel Thune?

A. No.

Q. Do you know that SFC Elwood is married?

A. Yes I do.

Q. At this time, are all the answers to the questions in this statement true?

A. Yes.

Q. Did PVT Ferguson ever sleep at your apartment?

A. I don't recall.

Q. Did PVT Ferguson ever come over to your apartment?

A. No.

Q. Why is it that this investigation disclosed that you had sex with Elwood and you are denying it?

A. Because I have no interest in going to bed with the man.

Q. What do you mean? You are not interested in males?

A. I don't have sex with men. I have sex with women.

Q. When was the last time you had sex with a woman, and what was her name?

A. It was Ferguson, in the billets in my room.

Q. How many other women have you had sex with while in the Army?

A. Two.

Q. OK, one was Ferguson. Who was the other one?

A. The other one was Michelle Levinson, who is a civilian, when I was at Fort Clementine, around November 1983.

Q. Did SFC Elwood ever go into your bedroom of your apartment here in West Germany?

A. No.

Q. Was there a New Year's party at your house?

A. No.

Q. Did you have anyone over your apartment on New Year's?

A. I went out.

Q. Who did you go out with?

A. I went out with some German girls.

Q. Were you at a gathering where the statements of the 15-6 investigation were passed around?

A. I don't recall.

Q. How many times have you been alone with SFC Elwood?

A. I can't recall.

Q. So are you telling me that you were only alone with women?

A. No. I'm not.

Q. If you can't recall, if you were alone and you are not stating that that you were with him, are you saying that you were never alone with Elwood?

A. I was never alone with Elwood.

Q. Did you ever commit oral sex upon SFC Elwood?

A. No.

Q. Did you ever kiss SFC Elwood?

A. No.

Q. Do you understand that if you are lying that you disobeyed the order from Major General Watters?

A. Yes, I do.

Q. Do you know PVT Ferguson?

A. Yes.

Q. Have you ever spoke with PVT Ferguson?

A. Yes.

Q. Did PVT Ferguson ever state who she was having sex with?

A. No, not to me.

Q. When was the last time you were alone with Elwood?

A. I can't recall, no time.

Q. Did you see any statements pertaining to this investigation?

A. Yes, the AR 15-6.

Q. What was on the statement pertaining to you and who showed it to you?

A. There were questions about me inviting her over to my house.

Q. Why is it that during our first interview, you stated over and over again, that PFC "Mackey" was not at your apartment and as soon as you entered this office you recall that she was?

A. Because you stated, "Ferguson."

Q. Did you telephone Elwood within the last three days?

A. No, I did not.

Q. Did you speak with Elwood within the last three days?

A. No.

Q. Is everything in this statement true?

A. No.

Q. What information is false?

A. Elwood has been to my apartment several times. While at the Thune we ate dinner, and a sex film was shown. I sometimes did call Elwood "Baby" and "Sweetheart." SFC Elwood was in my room while

I was on TDY at the Thune, but we only ate dinner in the room. Ferguson was at my house twice, and I am not gay, nor did I have sex with Ferguson or any other female. I was never really alone with SFC Elwood. SSG Smith was always with him, but the time in the Hotel Thune we were alone.

Q. Is everything else on the statement true, now?

A. Yes.

Q. Do you believe that you could have had sex with Elwood while you were drunk and that you can't recall the incident?

A. No.

Q. When was the last time you spoke to Elwood?

A. About two weeks ago on the phone, he called me.

Q. Did you engage in sexual acts with Elwood?

A. No.

Q. Was Ferguson, Mackey, or Smith at your apartment any time during the New Year's Eve night or New Year's Day?

A. No.

Q. Did SFC Elwood ever state that he was having sex with Leeds?

A. No.

Q. Did Elwood ever show you or state that there were pictures of him with Leeds having sex?

A. No.

Q. Do you understand that if you are not telling the truth about having sex with Elwood that you have committed a crime within the UCMJ?

A. Yes.

Q. Did you ever kiss Elwood as a friend at any time?

A. No, I never kissed him.

Q. Do you wish to add or delete anything in this statement?

A. No.

END OF STATEMENT

The Statement of SSG Albert Smith Follows:

I, SSG Albert Smith, **WANT TO MAKE THE FOLLOWING STATEMENT UNDER OATH:**

Q. SSG Smith, it has been brought to my attention that you have knowledge pertaining to the sexual activity of SFC Elwood, SP4 Leeds, and SGT Butler. Do you wish to discuss this, and if so please explain in your own words what you know?

A. I don't want to answer that question or make a statement. Well, I really didn't understand your question, but I wish to make a statement.

Q. Of the names mentioned above, did any of those individuals have sex that you know of?

A. Leeds mentioned to me that she had sex with SFC Elwood.

Q. When and where did she make this statement?

A. In the car coming from the guesthouse.

Q. Who was in the car when she said that?

A. Me, SFC Elwood, and SP4 Leeds.

Q. What did SFC Elwood state after SP4 Leeds told you she had sex with SFC Elwood?

A. He just looked and smiled.

Q. What happened at the guesthouse between SP4 Leeds and SFC Elwood?

A. They came into the room where I was with PVT Ferguson, and I said, "Let's have some fun." SP4 Leeds then took off her blouse; I pushed her on the bed, she fell on me, and I threw her off me. Then she took of her bra. Then I started to grab at PVT Ferguson. SP4 Leeds got mad and told me to leave her alone. PVT Ferguson then said she wanted something to drink, and then got mad and left. SP4 Leeds said Julia was getting drunk and acting like a fool. Then I started to get up and PVT Ferguson came back into the room. PVT Ferguson then said, "I'm going." Then she got her handbag. I got up and put my pants on. I then came back upstairs again to get Ferguson and they were fixing to leave. I then went back to bed. They went to their room and later came down and said, "Let's Go." So I drove them home.

Q. What were the exact words that SP4 Leeds stated to indicate that she had sex with Elwood?

A. She asked me where Ferguson was, and I told her I didn't know, she left, and then she joked by saying, "Do you miss your baby? Are you as big as Elwood?" SP4 Leeds said, "Julia said you are as big as Elwood but I don't think so." Then she started laughing.

Q. Is there any doubt in your mind that SFC Elwood didn't have sex with SP4 Leeds?

A. There is some doubt that he didn't, but I know SP4 Leeds. If she was in a room with him then she must have had sex with him.

Q. Did SFC Elwood ever state to you that he had sex with Leeds?

A. No. He didn't.

Q. Did SP4 Leeds ever state to you that she had sex with SFC Elwood?

A. No, she only said that he was big, meaning that I don't know.

Q. Why did that statement make you feel that SFC Elwood had sex with SP4 Leeds?

A. Because of what she said about him being big.

Q. Why does the description about SFC Elwood's being big indicate that they had sex?

A. Because I thought she was talking about his penis.

Q. SSG Smith, do you know if SFC Elwood ever had sex with SGT Butler?

A. No.

Q. SSG Smith, do you know if SFC Elwood had sex with any other person, not his wife?

A. No.

Q. Do you wish to add or delete anything to this statement?

A. No.

END OF STATEMENT

XHIBIT 15

In this investigation, the CID officers had PFC Mackey itled as a perpetrator. In Julia's personal opinion, Mackey hould have been titled as a victim due to her low rank as a private first class E-3 and due to her having been sexually exploited and prostituted by SSG Smith and SFC Elwood. She had also been deceived and taken advantage of by Sergeant Timmons, who was an E-5 and married. At the time he solicited her to have sexual relations with him. He knew better han to victimize her. He lied to her about his being single and then got her pregnant. She then discovered that he was married and continued to have relations with him for a few weeks afterward. PFC Mackey was granted immunity nevertheless and should have been absolved from being titled as a perpetrator in this case. Therefore justice was not served in his part of the case.

The Second Statement of PFC Lisa Mackey Follows:

I, PFC Lisa Mackey, **WANT TO MAKE THE FOLLOWING STATEMENT UNDER OATH:**

Q. PFC Mackey, do you fully understand that you were given an order to testify and testify truthfully before any agent of the United States Criminal Investigation

Command, pertaining to this investigation, and any thing you might say that could incriminate you wil not be used against you in any way, except for the prosecution for perjury, giving a false statement, o otherwise failing to comply with this order?

A. Yes.

Q. PFC Mackey, can you please explain, in your ow words, the information you have pertaining to thi investigation?

A. SP4 Timmons and I had sex about five or six times At the time I met him I didn't know he was married and then I found out a few weeks later, but the re lationship continued for a few weeks after that. We had sex or intercourse (nothing else) in my room, a night around seven or eight, in July or August 1984 That was it with SP4 Timmons. When I first arrivec here at C Company, 4th Support Battalion, APO NY 09031, SFC Elwood was introduced to me as my pla toon sergeant and he was real friendly toward me. I believe he was trying to get me to go to bed with him When we went over to Sergeant Butler's apartmen he was kissing on me—my mouth, my neck—and then he invited me to go to a concert at Fitzgeralc Air Base along with SSG Smith and PVT Ferguson I refused to go with him because I didn't think it was right. One night and on several occasions afterward,

SFC Elwood stated that his wife did what she wanted to do and that he could do what he wanted to do, meaning to me, having sex with me or anyone. After I refused to go with SFC Elwood to the concert in Fitzgerald, West Germany, things got hard for me.

He was rude to me in formation, making fun of me because I had asked him to repeat the information he had just talked about. He would go off on me and embarrass me in front of everyone.

Q. Who in your company that is involved in this investigation had sex with you?

A. Only SP4 Timmons.

Q. What do you know about a video or pictures of individuals in your unit performing sex acts?

A. I just heard that SP4 Leeds and Ferguson had heard about a video, that's all I know.

Q. Is there anything else that you could add to this statement pertaining to this investigation?

A. No.

END OF STATEMENT

CHAPTER X

———— ⌇⌇⌇ ————

THE CID INVESTIGATION CONCLUSION

After the CID investigation was concluded, the Judge Advocate General's Officers (JAGG) decided that the best course of action was to prosecute the said individuals, SFC Elwood and SSG Smith, with adultery, sodomy, prostitution and unlawful filming of sexual acts. SFC Elwood was sentenced to several years in Fort Leavenworth, Kansas, in federal prison and was dishonorably discharged from the US Army. SSG Smith was court-martialed, given a field grade Article 15 with reduced rank to SGT E-5, a one-thousand dollar fine with extra duty for one month, and then transferred to another unit in USAREUR. SFC Elwood was not allowed to collect his military retirement pension. SFC Elwood had been in the US Army for eighteen years and SSG Smith had been in the US Army for nineteen years. Both SFC Elwood and SSG Smith (especially due to his length of time in service) should have been dishonorably discharged for their reprehensible and disgraceful behavior respectively.

PFC Mackey was granted immunity for her testimony in the investigation. She was not charged with adultery and she was allowed to chapter out of the US Army based on a medical discharge due to her pregnancy with SP4 Timmons. SP4 Leeds and SGT Butler were both granted immunity for their knowledge and testimony in the CID investigation. Neither SP4 Leeds nor SGT Butler was charged with adultery.

On or about February 3, 1985, Julia was taken into a courtroom in the JAGG Building in Rheinhart, West Germany, and ordered to testify in court as to all of the incidents that happened with SSG Smith and SFC Elwood. Julia was instructed to answer the questions from the judge advocate in graphic detail while she was on the witness stand in that courtroom regarding her relationship with SSG Smith, SFC Elwood, SGT Butler, SP4 Leeds, and their involvement in these incidents.

SSG Smith's wife, who was of German descent, and SFC Elwood's wife, who was black, and an E-7, were both in the courtroom listening and watching Julia's testimony and the testimony of the others. This experience was not only embarrassing but mortifying to Julia as well. The expressions on their faces were incredulous. Their jaws dropped, and then they screamed, "You Slut! You home-wrecker! You have ruined our lives! You should be in jail!" Then the judge advocate had them permanently escorted out of the courtroom due to disrupting the court proceedings.

This was mind-blowing to Julia, since she had no idea from day to day what the plans of the CID/JAGG officers were going to be regarding the testimony of all of those involved in the CID investigation or the outcome of that process.

Subsequent to the court hearings, at or around 4:30 p.m., Julia was told that her mission was complete with CID and JAGG and that they had successfully obtained the information that they needed from her regarding her testimony in court. Julia was then escorted by one of the JAGG officers back to Howard Barracks to C Company in Rheinhart, where she was stationed temporarily until she was allowed to complete her ETS (end of time in service).

The JAGG officer instructed Julia not to discuss the case, court proceedings, or her leaving the company to any of the other soldiers in the barracks. Julia was instructed to pack up her belongings and to get ready to fly out of West Germany on the next military flight out of Fitzgerald Air Base, West Germany, at or around 2 a.m. on February 5, 1985.

So Julia packed up her belongings and stayed with a neutral female friend in her room down the hall. Julia was

varned about the possible repercussions of being terrorized
by PFC McPherson and her friends (who had, upon her ar-
ival to Howard Barracks and C Company, held her down
and beat the living daylights out of her, thus breaking her
nose and three of her ribs in the process) due to her spending
the last night at Howard Barracks at C Company.

On February 5, 1985 at 2 a.m. Julia was escorted to
Fitzgerald Air Base, West Germany, where she was then
given orders to board the military flight out of Germany to
Fort David, New Mexico, where she was stationed for one
day and out-processed with an honorable discharge from the
US Army. Julia had served her time, and what a long, strange
trip it had been indeed! Julia felt numb, scared, anxious, and
guarded. Upon her exit, there were no offers of any counseling or any support of any kind at all, only suggestions
to have her DD 214 paperwork copied and kept at the local Veterans Administration in Kellersville, Pennsylvania,
where she could summon a copy for employment purposes
in the future.

Julia's experience seemed as though she was just thrown
out like garbage after all the threats, physical abuse, and
trauma that she had suffered at the hands of some of the
highest-ranking individuals in the US Army. These were
the noncommissioned officers who were supposed to be
in charge and who were in positions of authority. Yet, they
abused their positions of power in the most disgusting,

dishonorable ways possible. Julia had no idea what her expe
rience in the US Army would do to her in terms of attracting
dysfunctional people, places, jobs, bosses, and situations
and how that would continue to play out the same experi
ence with a different twist.

Where military culture is concerned, the other parts o
the equation included the racial divide in the military cultur
as well as the alcoholism, drug addiction, sex addiction, etc
At the time that Julia was in the US Army, about 75 per
cent of the US Army consisted of African Americans and
Hispanics. Most of them enter at the enlisted level, joining
the US Army to find a home in which they belong due to be
ing socially isolated and economically disadvantaged youth

Between the 1960s and 1990s, many soldiers had the
choice to either join the US Army or to serve a jail sentence
for whatever misdemeanors—some of which were felony
convictions—that they had incurred. It was in Julia's experi
ence that she witnessed firsthand that military culture lends
itself to attract pedophiles, criminals, sexual predators, alco
holics and drug addicts, and neglected and abused children
These people join the US Army in their late teens in order
to find their way out of foster homes, dysfunctional, and/or
broken homes as well.

By the same token, one could find themselves in an out
standing unit regardless of what branch of the military one
joins. At the officer's level, less of this behavior is evident

since they must display leadership at all times, and is more discretely handled by the top brass if you will. The abuse and sexual exploitation is more apparent in the enlisted ranks of the military. Depending on what one is educated to bring into the military and what the commander is like in said units, it is possible for a military recruit to bypass this dysfunctional culture or to avoid getting caught up in it at all. The more educated one is, and the higher ranking at the officer's level, the more likely the influence will turn out in the opposite direction given what will take place, respectively. The tolerance for this dark side of the Army playing out all starts with the commanding officers at the top.

This experience is, again, based on a true story about the underhanded and dysfunctional abuse, sexual abuse, rape, stalking, and military sexual trauma that resulted in the traumatic experiences of a certain individual and those involved in this story. Unless one has walked a mile in that person's shoes, then no one has a right to judge the experience of that person. Let "He without sin cast the first stone," if you will. One must walk his or her own individual path in life. No one person is going to have the exact same experience as someone else in any given situation.

CHAPTER XI

—⬤⬤⬤—

THE EFFECTS AND PATTERNS OF MST AND TREATMENT

Julia's life story beyond the US Army unfolds to include the effects of military sexual trauma MST/PTSD for the next twenty-eight years until the present. Julia was twenty years old when she was released from the US Army. She is now fifty-two years old.

In Julia's case, her life proceeded to unfold as follows. After being honorably discharged for the US Army in early February 1985, Julia went home to live at her parents' house until she was able to stay with friends of hers in western New York State.

About two weeks later, Julia was invited by some friends who lived in Western Town, New York, to stay with them until she could find gainful employment. At the end of the first week, her friend Tricia and she went into town in Caribou, New York, and they each found jobs in retail stores almost immediately. Julia was hired at Hay Company and Tricia was hired at Mertz Department Store. Julia then met her first husband, Miles Freund, who would show her a level of love, sanctuary, and support that she had never known in her life.

Miles was also Julia's immediate boss at Hay Company. When his boss discovered that they were living together, Julia was told she had to go to work in a different department or else leave the company. So Julia was hired in the warehouse at Hay Company because that was most closely related to what she did in the US Army. Julia's drinking problem still existed and she had several bouts of depression and drunken episodes that cost her friends; she also almost lost her relationship with Miles, whom she was living with and whom she was engaged to be married to at that point.

After about six months of Miles tolerating Julia's alcoholism, he gave her an ultimatum, which was for Julia to get into treatment for alcoholism—to go to AA meetings—or he would kick her out. Julia couldn't blame him at all really. Julia agreed to follow through with that.

In October 1985 Julia's grandmother passed away from colon cancer while at her winter home in Florida. She was only seventy-two years old. Julia was very sad indeed. Julia's mother had offered to pay for her treatment in an alcohol rehabilitation center in another state. Julia agreed to go because she wanted to get sober and to get her life in order. Therefore, October 25, 1985 was the day Julia had taken her last alcoholic drink.

In early November 1985, Julia entered a 28 day rehabilitation center in Atlanta, Georgia. During her stay there, she met several nurses, doctors, pharmacists, lawyers, psychologists, and psychiatrists who were in treatment with her as patients themselves. Some of them were from Canada. Julia attended several group therapy sessions and she was able to "dump some of her emotional baggage" regarding her recent tour of duty in the US Army, and the sexual enslavement, rape, torture, and physical and emotional hell she had gone through.

The therapist, "Sherry," who ran the group in the afternoons was not real understanding of this and she blamed Julia for it. She stated, "You knew what you were doing because I used to work over there as a therapist in West Germany on an air force base. So don't say you were victimized, because you weren't!" Julia couldn't believe that her therapist would say that! She didn't argue with Sherry because she needed to talk about it. Julia did get some positive and validating feedback in group from two older retired military officers whom had been in the Navy.

Each of the retired admirals had said that Julia was a pawn in the game for the benefit of the noncommissioned officers who had sexually enslaved her and the other women involved and that it wasn't her fault at all. It wasn't until twenty-three years later that Julia would discover just how much in denial this therapist was in regarding the military sexual trauma she had experienced.

The post-traumatic stress disorder that Julia had, she had lived with for many years subsequent to that. (Post-traumatic stress disorder is defined as a very intense reliving of traumatic events that have happened in one's life. Distrust of other people is another issue. It also includes having several nightmares and flashbacks per week with the same theme over and over and over again. One tends to keep the lights on for most of the night, does not get regular sleep, is on automatic pilot, and one has trouble with authority figures.

One is also unable to deal with authority on any level and must either accept that jobs don't last or that one has a hard time respecting those in positions of authority directly over and above them. One does not like to be told what to do either. Therefore any employment is very spotty, or one must be engaged in one's own business and do things one's own way in direct relationships only. One must be in control of one's own path, per se.

Anyhow, at the end of November 1985, Julia completed the four weeks of rehabilitation required for her alcoholism.

Julia started going to several AA meetings per week and ob
tained two really great AA sponsors who were both highly
educated and motivated to assist her with working through
her AA Twelve-Step Program. Both of Julia's AA spon
sors were in training to become drug and alcohol therapists
Eventually Julia followed suit because she discovered he
gift as a clinical therapist as well.

On May 23, 1987, Julia married her first husband, Miles
Freund, in Kellersville, Pennsylvania. They married in the
Catholic Church and had their reception at an area inn, which
was lovely. Julia then moved to southern Pennsylvania with
Miles, outside the Marsburg area. On November 2, 1987
their daughter, Ariel L. Freund, was born.

During her early twenties Julia had been employed at
several jobs before and after she had Ariel. It seemed like
she constantly attracted people, places, and jobs that were a
repetitive pattern of the military sexual trauma she had ex
perienced in the US Army. These jobs did not last due to the
sexual harassment from coworkers and bosses that persisted
no matter what. Human resources in all of these companies
did not follow through on her filed complaints, so Julia end
ed up quitting these jobs. At the age of twenty-four Julia qui
a miserable state job as a file clerk because of the verbal
abuse and sexual harassment she suffered without any relief

Therefore, in May of 1989, after Julia and Miles had just
purchased their first home in Marsburg, Pennsylvania, Julia

resigned from the Pennsylvania state agency she worked at in order to start her own residential cleaning business. Shortly beforehand, Julia's daughter, Ariel, was diagnosed as special needs at the age of eighteen months. Ariel is developmentally delayed and autistic. This diagnosis and special need for care placed her in a category that meant Miles and Julia would have to work with her as parents for much of her life.

During Ariel's formative years, Julia wanted to balance out spending time with Ariel with going to college to get a degree, so she pursued that goal. However, as Julia grew into her own person she stayed sober, yet she wasn't the person that Miles expected her to be.

Therefore, Miles and Julia grew apart and were granted a divorce on October 17, 1991. They hired an attorney, who drew up a contractual agreement with terms of shared custody of Ariel, no child support, and no lawyers involved. This was a 90-day no-fault divorce filed during the summer of 1991, which became final in October 1991. They then placed the house on the market for sale, effective immediately. Miles moved out of their home in August 1991.

In November 1991, after Ariel's fourth birthday, Julia began dating a man named Bill, whom she had met in AA. He was eighteen years older than she was and turned out to be a pedophile! He and Julia split up after about six weeks because she could not trust him around her daughter, Ariel. Bill had also been in therapy for his own sex addiction and then went into a rehabilitation facility in New Orleans, Louisiana, for his own intensive treatment.

Then, in January 1992, Julia met a man named Kyle whom she met in AA and began dating for several months. Initially, Julia could not understand why he always strayed from her to dance with other women while they were out dancing and why he always watched and read pornographic material. It seemed that he was never satisfied with just one woman. Since they both had a sexual hook, they stayed together, even after Julia had discovered that he cheated on her with another woman one night at the area club they would frequent! Julia allowed Kyle to treat her like a sexual toy and he was emotionally unavailable to her on a regular basis. He was however, very good with Ariel and loved spending time with her when she was little. Julia trusted him with her and knew she was safe. He really had no goals in life other than to stay sober and go to AA meetings. Kyle worked at a menial job as a nursing assistant on third shift making minimum wage and did not wish to educate himself further. He really had nothing to offer Julia either.

Julia then purchased a very nice mobile home shortly after her house sold in August 1992. Therefore, Julia went to college and then to graduate school. The only saving grace otherwise was that Kyle's family was very good to both Julia and Ariel. Kyle's parents and his brothers were wonderful to them and this was like the family Julia never had, so she did her best to try and "fix" Kyle and his behavior. Julia's self-esteem was very low at that time and therefore she didn't think she was worth any more than that.

Here, Julia had attracted a sex addict whom she became sexually codependent with for many years to follow! In early fall of 1992, Julia's cleaning business was hitting a bottom financially, and therefore, she had to do something else. At the time Julia had partial custody of Ariel with her dad, Miles, who lived about twenty minutes from them. Julia was feeling very depressed and went to see her family doctor, who put her on Prozac for a year.

During that time, in March 1993, Julia never thought she would do something like this but she applied for and was hired on as a stripper at Adult World in Marsburg, Pennsylvania. This lasted about six months. Julia felt a sense of control over her body and her life. Julia had lots of fun and she made great money and felt on top of the world! No one was allowed to put their hands on any of the girls who worked at Adult World either. Kyle knew about and managed the money Julia made as well. He promoted this acting out behavior on Julia's part because it fed his sex addiction. Julia believed that this continued as a cemented way of behavior that she learned from being prostituted in the US Army.

During that summer, Julia was hired on at another Pennsylvania state agency in June 1993 to attend several months of training during the day and to become a county caseworker. After three months, Julia failed that training miserably!

Then Julia and two other women who worked at Adult World got fired because the owner thought that they appeared to look too fat! Therefore, Julia was grateful that she was able to help them to get sober and into AA and Al-Anon Meetings. Shortly after that chapter ended in October 1993, Julia went to work as an escort at a local escort service for men. Julia made great money, but she felt totally ashamed of herself for doing this. It seemed like she was a counselor to these men, who constantly complained that their wives did not pay attention to them or that they were just never satisfied with one woman. Julia was fortunate not to get arrested, raped, or killed during this phase of her life either, thank God!

In March 1994 Julia left that profession and made a vow to herself and to God that she would do anything she was qualified to do and finish her college education no matter what!

In May 1994 Julia graduated with her Associate's Degree in Liberal Arts from Hogan Community College. She went back to her cleaning business, and then landed a job as a nursing home social worker just down the road. Then Julia applied to Benz State University to pursue her Bachelor's Degree in Applied Behavioral Science so she could go on to become a clinical therapist. After Julia graduated from Benz tate University, she got a job as an entry-level drug and alcohol counselor about an hour away. It only paid just above minimum wage and was only part-time. After learning of the welfare fraud that the agency was involved in, Julia resigned our months later in August 1996. Julia had applied to and been accepted at East Coast University to begin her master's degree program in education. This was an Adult Education and Group Process Master's Degree that held more weight for her and where she felt more accepted and did very well indeed! Julia enjoyed that program, and after graduating in January 1998, Julia still worked in her cleaning business and in some temporary jobs. Julia then decided that it was time to get out of the Marsburg area if she was going to have a chance at her dream career master's level therapist.

Out of convenience, Kyle and Julia stayed in the relationship to take advantage of their roommate-like relationship for Ariel's sake and for their own individual goals that they both had. Kyle and Julia moved from the trailer in September 1999 to rent a house just outside of Banshee, Pennsylvania. At that time Julia had landed a job in Washburn, Pennsylvania as a master's level clinical therapist at a very prestigious rehabilitation center.

Julia left Ariel with her dad because that is what he wanted and it worked well for Ariel in terms of having stability and a daily routine. Julia just continued to get Ariel on the weekends and on school vacations and holidays.

The position at the rehabilitation center only lasted two months because Julia's boss told her that she had the "kind of energy that could incite riots" and to meet him in his office after hours or lose her job. He began to sexually harass her and threaten her with losing her job if she didn't get together with him. Therefore, after avoiding him several times Julia quit and left her job after two months into it. Julia had no recourse because she wasn't there long enough to fight for her job or to collect unemployment. Next, Julia was able to get another job as an assistant director of education at a local vocational school. The same pattern ensued; Julia's boss started to sexually harass her and threaten her with being fired if she didn't do as he said. Therefore, Julia reported it to his boss, who then fired her for no reason. Then Julia applied for unemployment and won because she did nothing wrong. Julia also filed a lawsuit against the company and won with a small settlement out of court.

During that time, in May 2000, Julia applied to graduate school to a doctoral program in clinical psychology at Frazer University in Waldorf, Pennsylvania. Julia also applied for a contract position as an independent therapist at Women's Coaching Services in Banshee, Pennsylvania.

Julia obtained both the job, to begin in May 2000, and then was invited by her advisor at Frazer University to accept a space in the doctoral program to begin in September 2000! Yay! Julia finally got somewhere!

At this point, Julia was working two jobs, the other being a wraparound mobile therapist to work with children who had been diagnosed with behavioral disorders in the community, schools, and in their homes. So her life at that time was very full very quickly!

Julia was elated that she could finally be in her element and really engage life in a way that worked well for her! In late September 2000, Julia and Kyle moved out of the house they had rented in Washburn, Pennsylvania, and then rented one in Silverton, Pennsylvania.

In July 2000, and during this time, Kyle had obtained a job as an aid on the adolescent unit of the same rehab that Julia worked at about nine months prior to that. He only lasted about three months because he was using the computer at work on the night shift to view animal pornography. The rehab software systems administrators had tracked his every move online and had viewed his pornographic choices for two weeks. They turned him in to the administrators, who suspended him for three days and then proceeded to fire him for his sex addiction online in October 2000. They told him that they thought he had a serious problem and needed to seek help for his sex addiction.

At that point, Julia asked him to leave and to "get out" because she had had enough of his crap with respect to his sex addiction. He would constantly view pornography online, exchange naked pictures of himself with other women and their body parts in an email, and/or engage in online cybersex in a chat room over the internet.

Kyle refused to leave and promised to get some help by going to counseling for his sex addiction. He only went to two counseling sessions and that was it!

With no job, Julia suggested that he work for a temporary agency as a nursing assistant until he could find a permanent full-time job again. Julia supported them while that went on. Kyle then was hired permanently at the county nursing home for a third shift position to start in March 2001. During that time Julia worked like hell in school and at work. Julia's jobs were only hourly, as an independent contractor with no benefits. Julia needed the flexibility so she could attend graduate school at Frazer University. Things went on like this until Women's Coaching Services closed in April 2002. In August 2002, Julia was hired as an independent contract therapist at Forensics Counseling Services in Peyton, Pennsylvania. During this time, Kyle and Julia moved into separate bedrooms because the relationship had since deteriorated badly.

In the fall of 2003, Julia discovered that Kyle had been openly cheating on her with other women by finding a prophylactic in his car. When Julia confronted him with it, he slammed his bedroom door in her face and denied it.

Julia knew at that point that no matter what she needed to get a full-time job with benefits so she could support herself and purchase her own vehicle in her own name. Therefore, in February 2003 Julia was lucky enough to be hired at Moon Day Children's Centers at the office in Banshee, Pennsylvania. Julia had a full-time flexible job as a behavioral therapist/mobile therapist with benefits. In late February 2003, Kyle and Julia filed their tax returns together, which they did every year because they always got the best tax breaks when they did that. That night, he took off and met some girl at the adult bookstore downtown in Banshee, Pennsylvania. They spent the night together and Julia found out because she discovered a receipt for makeup under the seat of his car the next day. Julia confronted him with it and he admitted to it. Julia was angry and very upset about it, yet somehow it didn't surprise her at all given his history.

Julia then worked toward getting her credit back in order so she could get her own car and get out from underneath having a car loan with Kyle. Their 1996 Ford Thunderbird was just about paid off when Julia decided to buy her own brand new car in June 2003 at the local Honda Dealership. Julia got the best deal ever! Julia felt like she was finally getting some freedom and independence back! Therefore, she was so very happy when she did this for herself and by herself without Kyle signing his name with her on the title and without Julia's being stuck with his name on the loan either. Both Julia and Kyle wanted to get out of the relationship and they knew it would take some more time in order for that to happen. In October 2003 Julia discovered that their relationship was no longer recognized as a common-law marriage in the State of Pennsylvania.

Julia had to decide that she no longer wanted live with Kyle and that she was going to leave him and get her own apartment elsewhere. At that time Julia had been chatting with single men online because she wanted to see who might be interested in dating her at some point. Even though Julia did not go out with anyone, it was nice to get to know some people. Kyle got suspicious and then got so angry and possessive after going through Julia's email! He threatened her with taking all of her belongings and throwing them out into the street.

Early in November 2003 Julia was picking up her daughter Ariel for the weekend in Moynihan, Pennsylvania, which was over an hour away from Silverton, Pennsylvania. At that point Julia ended up calling the regional police and alerting them to her situation. One of the officers called her back and assured her that he had gone over to the house in Silverton and warned Kyle not to touch Julia's computer, not to throw out her clothing, or to threaten her or Ariel in any way, shape, or form or that he would be going to jail.

The officer told Julia that if Kyle's behavior continued that she should file an emergency restraining order against him immediately. After that night, Julia realized that she needed to have a plan in place to get out and to protect herself from Kyle. So Julia asked her dad for some financial assistance so she could get enough money to move out of the house and into her own apartment. Julia called their landlord on November 14, 2003, and told her that she was going to leave Kyle and that she could not spend another Christmas with him because it was just miserable! The landlord became angry because she wanted forty-five days of notice to vacate even though they had lived in the house for over three years and they were on a month-to-month lease at that point. So they agreed to compromise and that Julia and Kyle would move out on December 15, 2003.

They each did that and Julia was able to get her own apartment in Herschel, Pennsylvania. Kyle ended up moving in with a drunk who lived on the other side of town in Silverton, Pennsylvania.

That arrangement only lasted six weeks and then Julia was foolish enough to buy into Kyle's ranting and raving that "she owed him" for all the years he had worked while Julia went to school. Well, Julia worked also and lived on student loans and money that her mom had given to them as well. Julia had to pay back the student loans also. Julia took care of Kyle, cleaned the house, did the laundry, made his meals, cooked, etc. Julia did her share and then some. Therefore, neither one of them owed the other anything, as far as Julia was concerned. They were not legally married, had no children and had no assets together at that point.

Therefore, with some stipulations, such as Kyle's will
ingness to quit his miserable job and go to nursing schoo
and see a psychiatrist and go to couples counseling, Juli
thought that they could try again to set about making thi
work for them.

Kyle agreed to all of these stipulations and Julia allowe
him to move in with her to see if they could make a go of i
once again. Kyle's family was always wonderful to Julia an
Ariel, therefore it was hard for them to let go of the dysfunc
tional relationship Julia had with Kyle for so many years be
cause his parents and siblings were like the family she neve
had really.

Anyhow, Kyle went to see a psychiatrist who blame
Julia for their troubles, and then Kyle refused to go to coun
seling or to quit his job and go to school. Therefore, afte
about two months, Julia told him he would have to get hi
act together or leave.

In February 2004 Julia was being sexually stalked and ha
rassed by her immediate supervisor at Moon Day Children'
Centers, who happened to be female. She showed up on thei
doorstep on Valentine's Day evening with a rose in her hand
Julia invited her in and told her she was not interested in tha
kind of relationship with her. She left and got angry wit
Julia. Then she started harassing Julia about her paperworl
and any mistakes she made. The boss was targeting Julia a
well. Therefore, Julia had no choice but to leave her job o

get fired. So Julia took three weeks of sick leave and vacation from about mid-February until early March 2004. On March 4, Julia began a weight-loss program, which began to work wonders for her. Julia ended up losing thirty pounds on L.A. Weight Loss. Julia got a fabulous haircut and felt herself transform into a different person.

Then on March 9, 2004, Julia resigned from her job because of the sexual harassment from her boss. Julia then went to an administrative hearing at the UC Office in Ellenville, Pennsylvania. The judge told her that even though the boss was out of line for doing that, Julia did not put up with her behavior long enough for it to be considered sexual harassment. Therefore Julia lost that hearing and she could not collect unemployment. So Julia scrambled to find her next job, which she was unsuccessful in doing. Julia did part-time tarot readings on the side, which put groceries on the table, but that was it. Julia was close to having spent most of her savings, therefore, she still relied on Kyle for the time being.

Then, in May 2004, Julia was involved in a car accident where she was struck by another car from behind. Julia's car was in the shop for almost three weeks.

On May 21st, her friend, Lorraine Stirling from work at Moon Day Children's Centers, asked Julia to join her for dinner on May 23rd, 2004 at Maude Stiring's house. Lorraine wanted Julia to meet this man, Charles Robert Stirling, from Texas. Maude was Charles Stirling's sister. Julia was not looking to meet anyone at that time.

However, Julia knew it was over between her and Kyle and that he would have to get out sooner rather than later. Julia told him to pack his belongings and to leave because there was no point in staying together. Kyle did put up a fight verbally, but took the initiative to get his own apartment and he finally left. It took a restraining order from the court to get him to leave Julia alone!

That young naïve US Army Private E-1, who had lived and grown personally through all of this, was me; I was living this incredible story! Now, I share my experience, strength, and hope so that I can benefit other people.

CHAPTER XII

---—◦◦◦◦—---

PERSONAL GROWTH AND DEVELOPMENT

On May 23, 2004, I met my soul mate, Charles Robert Stirling, "Charlie" whom I have now been married to for thirteen years! It is now October 11, 2017, as I finish writing this book!

In the several years subsequent to my experience with military sexual trauma in the US Army, which began for me at the age of twenty, I continued to attract dysfunctional people, places, and situations, including bosses, due to my unaddressed issues of military sexual trauma that affected me for many years and are ongoing to this day.

Finally, in August 2006, I was encouraged by my husband, Charlie, to seek help at the local VA so as to address my ongoing issues with military sexual trauma and related post-traumatic stress disorder. At this time we had moved to Texas, where there were limited resources. We had lost almost everything. We were also homeless and in the process of moving back to Pennsylvania at that time. I was fortunate enough to have met a very well informed retired female US Air Force lieutenant colonel, who was on my staff at the county offices where I worked as a supervisor. She said to me on a regular basis, "Julia, you need to get your ass over to the VA so you can address your issues!" It was not until November 2007 that I was able to finally get to the VA in Ellenville, Pennsylvania, to seek and receive help for these issues.

It turned out that I had been struggling with PTSD for many years and had no idea that this is what created such dysfunctional patterns of behavior for me in terms of attracting dysfunctional relationships with people, including bosses, places, and situations on a regular basis.

My employment history had taken an ugly turn for the worst and therefore, I was able to see this pattern as it played out. The chief of psychiatry at the VA Outpatient Center had suggested that I file for permanent disability with the VA because this pattern would only serve to destroy me further emotionally. Therefore, I filed for permanent disability on July 7, 2008, and had done all of the legwork to collect and submit the paperwork and several pages of documentation via CID report to the Veterans' Administration in a nearby own called New Croatia, Pennsylvania, with the Vietnam Veterans' War Coalition.

In March 2009 I was sent to the VA Medical Center in New Croatia, Pennsylvania, to undergo psychological testing with the VA Compensation and Pension Department. Immediately upon having taken those tests with the psychologist, I was awarded 100 percent permanent disability by the VA based on the ongoing and continuous MST-related PTSD that I suffer from.

As I look back on my US Army experience and my spotty employment history, I can see now all of the patterns of this puzzle, and how it all makes sense now. In looking back on my experience in the US Army, and in comparing it to what is happening now in the US Military, and in society in general, not much has changed really. The same sexual exploitation, stalking, and rape happened as it did then over thirty years ago. The only difference is that there have been public newscasts about class-action law suits, and disgraced people in high positions of power and authority in society. Both officers and noncommissioned officers in the military having been charged with these same crimes were prosecuted.

In order to change the good-old-boy culture, the entire system must be gutted from the ground floor and revised according to the fair accountability, responsibility, respect, and integrity that each individual soldier, both male and female, deserves to be treated with on a regular basis.

AFTERWORD

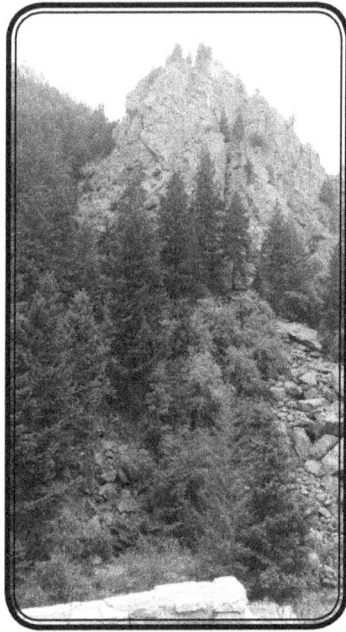

The View From the Mountain Top!

It is my sincerest hope that my story will indeed inspire others in this audience to come forward and feel safe in sharing their stories, experience, strength, and hope, so that all of us who are disabled veterans can come together and bond in knowing that we are not alone. There is indeed help and on-going treatment for symptom management, and for the per-manent scars and post-traumatic stress disorder that never seem to go away. May we all heal in the light and rise again like the phoenix rising from the ashes!

May all of us who have been afflicted with and suffer from military sexual trauma-related post-traumatic stress disorder have the courage to stand in our own truth as the brave people that we are! It is not what happens to us in life. It is how we react to and deal with it.

This mountain that I have personally climbed now af-fords me the view from the top! My entire journey is indeed a truly major and colorful Tapestry of Life.